New Models
for
Higher Education

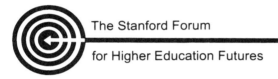

The Stanford Forum

for Higher Education Futures

Joel W. Meyerson and William F. Massy
Editors

Peterson's

Princeton, New Jersey

Composition and design by Peterson's

ISBN 1-56079-808-4

Printed in the United States of America

10 9 8 7 6 5 4 3 2 1

Contents

::

Preface   **vii**

1 ::: Industrial Strength Academies   **1**
      Henry E. Riggs

2 ::: Leveraged Learning: Technology's Role in
Restructuring Higher Education   **19**
      Sally V. Massy

3 ::: University of Pennsylvania Health System Model:
The Academic Health Center As the Nucleus of an
Intgrated Health Care Delivery System   **37**
      William N. Kelley, MD

4 ::: From Shared Governance to Shared Responsibility:
The Great and Painful Labor of Adaptation Has Begun   **65**
      Stephen Joel Trachtenberg

5 ::: Rethinking Academic Structures   **85**
      Jillinda Kidwell and David O'Brien

6 ::: Simulating the Academy: Toward Understanding
Colleges and Universities as Dynamic Systems   **107**
      *Jesse H. Ausabel, Robert Herman, William F. Massy
and Sally V. Massy*

7 ::: Budget Equilibrium Model   **121**
      Jon C. Strauss

8 ::: Recasting the Oregon State System   **129**
      Weldon E. Ihrig

Contributors   **141**

Preface

The Stanford Forum is a national research center resident at Stanford University. It sponsors and conducts research on issues likely to influence the future of higher education, principally in strategy, finance, management and technology. It presents and discusses research in annual symposia, retreats and round-tables with campus leaders and other decision-makers and disseminates findings and proceedings through books, monographs, and articles.

The Stanford Forum is composed of roughly 150 thought leaders from across the country, including senior financial and administrative officers, trustees and academic researchers. The Stanford Forum has been resident at Stanford University since 1990. Prior to moving to Stanford, the Forum was resident at Columbia University for six years, starting with its inception in 1984, where it was known at the Forum for College Financing at Columbia. The Forum was originally funded by a five-year grant from the U.S. Department of Education. Since 1990, it has been privately funded by a small number of business, professional and nonprofit organizations.

Most of the papers that appear in this volume were presented at recent symposia of the Stanford Forum; others were published as monographs by the Forum or authored by Forum members specifically for this book.

Funding to support the Stanford Forum is provided by Coopers & Lybrand, Goldman Sachs & Co., International Business Machine, Morgan Stanley & Co., Inc., Lehman Brothers, NACUBO, Prager, McCarthy & Sealy, and United Educators, Inc.

Chapter 1

::

Industrial Strength Academies

Henry E. Riggs, **Harvey Mudd College**

::

Why can't higher education operate more like business? College and university presidents will likely recognize this familiar lament—they hear it often, especially from corporate executives serving on their governing boards. Indeed, as educator Richard Chait has observed, "The most influential management models for higher education derive principally from the corporate sector. Whether correct or not, conventional wisdom holds that businesses are better managed than colleges and universities."[1]

Yet veteran management professor Peter Drucker points out that "in the most crucial area—the motivation and productivity of knowledge workers—[nonprofit organizations] are truly pioneers, working out the policies and practices that business will have to learn tomorrow."[2]

It is clear to me, having served as university professor and development officer, corporate chief executive, and now as college president, that certain organizational practices in either realm—industry or

---

[1] "The New Activism of Corporate Boards and the Implications for Campus Governance," Occasional Paper No. 26, Association of Governing Boards of Universities and Colleges, Spring 1995.
[2] "What Business Can Learn from Nonprofits," *Harvard Business Review*, July–August 1989.

1

academe—can be usefully adopted by the other. For although different in some fundamental and important ways, the two worlds are more similar than conventional thinking might lead us to believe.

The contrast between the archetypal "picture postcard" college—small, residential, liberal arts—and the heavy industrial plant with its billowing smokestacks is indeed stark. But academic institutions like these educate less than 10 percent of today's undergraduates and smokestack industries comprise a sharply decreasing share of the nation's economic activity. Large universities now dominate undergraduate instruction, and service and light manufacturing operations—increasingly high-tech and high-touch—represent the wave of the for-profit future.

Likewise, the jobs of college president and industrial captain, substantially different a half-century ago, are growing more alike. The parallels are particularly striking between academic leaders and leaders of technology-intensive industrial companies whose success depends upon a large cadre of highly educated, creative, and independent professionals (e.g., pharmaceutical, biotechnology, software, semiconductor, and electronic instrumentation firms). This likeness was underscored for me when I recognized that the articles I find most thought-provoking and helpful in my present position as an academic president come from the business rather than the academic press.

Before my academic colleagues dismiss me as just another industrial type seeking to impose for-profit methods on not-for-profit activities, let me agree quickly that many industrial organization models and processes of control, management, and leadership are not directly transferable to the academic world. I would not argue that academic presidents should necessarily be recruited from industry. Rather I would argue that leaders in both realms might benefit by erasing some of the differences that persist between them rather than blindly accepting such differences.

Several profound external forces are reshaping both sets of institutions. As these forces cause internal behaviors (or methods and practices, if you like) to change, the organizational cultures of both worlds are being substantially altered and are growing more alike. Leaders of these organizations can strengthen them by understanding and selectively applying practices from each other's realm.

EXTERNAL FORCES

Industrial companies and academic institutions both prosper or falter in the same economic, societal, and governmental environment—an environment in which the forces of change are formidable. These forces buffet colleges and companies in similar ways and are a primary cause of the convergence in the challenges facing both sets of leaders. Among the conditions precipitating profound change are:

- rapidly changing markets
- heightened competition
- an avalanche of new technologies
- increased demand for accountability

Rapidly Changing Markets

Rapidly changing markets are an article of faith in today's business environment. Consequently, companies are much more zealous than they once were about getting close to their customers and understanding their needs. Corporate strategy and capabilities are unambiguously focused on customer satisfaction.

Belatedly, academic institutions are awakening to realize that they too operate in markets—several markets, in fact—and that these markets are rapidly changing also. Higher education is following in business's footsteps by intensifying its customer focus. Conveniently, its various markets—the faculty and staff labor markets, student recruitment market, philanthropic market, research funding market, credit market, and job placement market—are providing feedback in ways and at decibel levels not previously encountered. Those in higher education may not be sanguine about everything they hear, but their response should be the same as the industrial marketing manager's: Get close to customers (in academe's case: students, government, donors, etc.), understand their needs, and match them to the needs of the institution.

Shifting enrollment demographics are changing the student market dramatically. Nontraditional learners, the fastest growing market segment, are older, more diverse in background and preparation, and less likely to reside on campus or attend class full-time. Institutions will need to tailor their marketing strategies to appeal to this broader range of needs and sensitivities.

Certain student demands are transcending individual market segments. One such demand is the call for colleges, and especially universities, to pay increased attention to the undergraduate. Several institutions are addressing this concern by developing honors colleges and other colleges-within-the-university. Market pressure to level tuition rates or, at a minimum, sharply decelerate them is also mounting. Recent data indicate that colleges and universities are gradually responding by keeping cost-rise closer to inflation rates and by engaging in price discounting.

The research market in which higher education operates is also changing. Traditionally, faculty have been able to define their own agendas and then seek external funding. Increasingly, however, to ensure a greater chance of success as fiscal resources become more constrained, faculty try to anticipate the interests of both public and private funding sources and design their proposals accordingly. The growing number of Washington, D.C.–based satellite offices established by research universities is one sign of higher education's intensified interest in encouraging communication with its patrons—in this case, America's single largest funder of basic research, the federal government. Defense, aerospace, and other industry contractors have maintained similar offices for years.

The private philanthropic market is demanding more influence and control over how its dollars are spent as well. An academic institution's ability to raise unrestricted funds—funds spent at the administration's discretion—has become considerably more difficult. Restricted gifts, where the donor designates use, now comprise about 90 percent of the aggregated gift receipts of colleges and universities.

Academe and industry are jointly struggling to respond appropriately in a marketplace where they both provide services—the health-care industry. Conditions in this arena have been sharply altered in the past several years by regulatory and economic forces.

Heightened Competition

Competition for customers openly exists in the business world and has only intensified with the arrival of global markets and suppliers. Competition for students in the academic world, on the other hand, has appeared minimal until recently. Now, however, such competition is surfacing openly and aggressively in the unabashed behavior of certain colleges and universities. The reason? Except at the most elite academic institutions—where a recent surge of brand-name consumerism has resulted in record numbers of worthy applicants—admissions officers are increasingly challenged by the difficulty of attracting the best possible students. Many are resorting to a blizzard of discounted tuition schemes, including a variety of merit scholarships and "pay-for-four-get-five-years" plans. At some enrollment-driven institutions, published tuition rates serve only as "sticker prices" that indicate where bargaining begins.

Competition for research dollars among academic institutions has also grown fiercer due to diminished support from federal agencies and industrial research labs. And in the philanthropic market, social agencies and cultural institutions that have historically relied on government funding are now siphoning away at least some of the private support that might otherwise have landed at higher education's doorstep. Moreover, private higher education institutions are now having to contend with competition from public counterparts who, as state budgets shrink, more actively pursue private gifts. Some publics have developed fund-raising operations that now rival privates in scope and sophistication. The current leapfrogging by one institution over another to initiate and then extend record-breaking campaigns reflects the intensity of the battle. Increased demand for their services has already created a shortage of talented, responsible, and experienced development officers in academe.

An Avalanche of New Technologies

Leaders in both industry and academe are struggling to understand and apply in a cost-effective manner an avalanche of new computer and communications technologies.

The technology emphasis in industry has been on lowering costs to increase productivity. But leaders are coming to realize that productivity can also rise by simply using technology to improve quality even if costs are kept constant and not reduced.

In higher education, the promise of quality improvement is what clearly motivates most faculty who adopt new technologies. The term "productivity," especially when linked with "teaching," remains anathema among the professoriate, who erroneously associate it with quality loss. Some academic administrators, under increasing financial pressures, unfortunately reinforce this notion by presenting cost reduction rather than quality improvement as the key reason for infusing technology into instruction.

A key challenge for leaders in both academe and industry is to realize for themselves—and then to educate their organizations—that productivity and quality are not competing priorities but rather parts of the same equation, and that increased productivity can be achieved in a number of ways that maintain or increase quality.

Increased Demand for Accountability

The world has long empathized with college and university leaders in their struggles to cater to multiple constituencies—students, parents, faculty, trustees, alumni, staff, donors, lenders, research funders, government regulators, state appropriations committees, and the like. Indeed, the need to orchestrate the conflicting demands of these many constituencies is cited as a major factor in differentiating the academic president's job from that of his or her industrial counterpart.

But industry is progressively moving in the direction of the academy. One hears increasingly that companies must be responsive to stakeholders as well as shareholders. Such stakeholders include employees, the community, government regulators, suppliers, joint venture and alliance partners, and customers.

In other cases, the demand for greater accountability is driving academic practices closer to those of business. One promising example is the demand from academic trustees for greater fiscal accountability that is leading some institutions to modify or eliminate traditional fund accounting, a method that obscures far more than it ever illuminates.

SHARED MANAGEMENT: CHALLENGES AND RESPONSES

Given that the same external forces affect both industry and academe, one might expect the operational changes underway in both worlds—changes in the ways in which activities are managed—to be similar. Indeed, the similarities in management practices are now more striking than the differences. Divergent vocabulary may be used to describe these practices, but the organizational assumptions that underlie them and the day-to-day behavioral changes they elicit are very much the same. Furthermore, the management challenges and responses that higher education shares with industry are not confined to administrative support areas but extend to the academic core—teaching and research. They include:

- empowerment
- the struggle between short and long term
- decentralization
- labor constraints
- the "not invented here" syndrome
- the recruitment process
- leading versus managing

Empowerment

Empowerment requires top management to share the key tasks of setting direction, seeking continuous improvement, and evaluating results with colleagues throughout an organization. Although industry has come to recognize the benefits of devolving authority and responsibility—to such an extent that the term empowerment borders on corporate cliché—it took a long time for Taylorism, the practice of "programming" employees to be efficient, to be abandoned in favor of the obvious: The person who performs a task is usually best positioned to determine how to do it better.

Higher education, on the other hand, has practiced the concept of empowerment for generations under the rubric "shared governance." Academic leaders have long acknowledged that an institution's strength lies in its faculty—those who do the line work of teaching and research. Not only are faculty usually the source of the best new ideas, they are given the ultimate responsibility for implementing new initiatives.

To the extent that a company has highly competent and dedicated employees—from officers to scientists and technologists, to marketing directors, to the rank and file—those employees expect to similarly share in key decision making. They expect shared governance for precisely the same reasons that faculty insist on it. Biotechnology chief executives are about as unlikely to dictate to their research scientists exactly what investigative paths to follow as academic presidents are to outline a faculty member's precise scholarly research or the syllabus for a particular course.

There is a difference to be sure. Tradition and constitutions mandate that academic presidents seek the counsel and advice of faculties on virtually all key matters (not solely those affecting curriculum, pedagogy, and research), whereas industrial leaders retain the option to empower and generally do so regarding a more limited set of corporate issues.

Empowerment in the academy extends to students as well. Old traditions of "command and control" teaching—i.e., lecturing to the students and then testing them on the lectures—are giving way to new pedagogies that encourage students to take responsibility for their own learning and place faculty in the roles of coaches, mentors, and even collaborators.

Teaming is another form of empowerment that takes place in both industry and academe. The use of teams in business for problem solving, product development, and marketing strategies is spreading enormously. In academe, where committees grow like weeds, those constituted as task forces—with specific and consequential goals, defined time frames, and distinctly different membership roles—are simply teams by another name. Industry's response to a challenge or problem is increasingly to set up a team; the academic world inevitably forms a faculty committee: the behaviors are similar.

The Struggle Between Short and Long Term

Industry is frequently and vehemently criticized for overemphasizing next quarter's earnings per share. The argument goes that too many companies sacrifice the long term—research, market development, modernizing facilities—to the expediency of near-term profits. On the other hand, the long term is irrelevant unless the company and, to be honest, the managers themselves survive the short term. The key is balance. Every industrial leader knows this, but developing consensus on what constitutes the proper balance is no simple matter.

The academy is roundly criticized for over-emphasizing faculty research and shortchanging teaching activities, particularly undergraduate instruction. Substitute the phrase "scholarly activity" for research—an appropriate substitution for many faculty members—and the teaching–research issue becomes one of short-term vs. long-term priorities. As in industry, balance is the key. Faculty members who are outstanding classroom teachers must remain intellectually active and alert to sustain their teaching excellence. As teaching becomes less an activity of lecturing and more one of mentoring or coaching, faculty dedication to building intellectual capital becomes especially critical.

Decentralization

As companies and universities grow, they tend to decentralize. As they diversify into increasingly heterogeneous activities, decentralization is extended. In industry, companies evolve from functional organizations to separate divisions, then to groups. In time, the corporation may come to resemble a holding company.

Colleges and universities evolve from academic departments to separate schools within the university, perhaps even to multiple campuses. The individual units become more and more heterogeneous. Activities in the School of Arts and Sciences' English department are vastly different from those in the School of Medicine's cardiology department, as are those of physics from those of physical education.

Arguably, decentralization challenges the academic leader more than it does his or her industrial counterpart, since large research and land-grant universities pursue substantially less focused missions than do giant multi-industry, multinational corporations. Ask any university president where the power, authority, and resources on campus reside on his or her campus. They are in the schools, particularly the professional schools, and in the athletic department—units that excel at raising their own funds, be it from gifts, research funding, or gate receipts. These units resent the "tax" they are often required to pay to the central administration for being part of the university. The business school dean's office may be across the street from the president's but sometimes, in terms of organizational distance, it may as well be in Tokyo or Karachi!

Decentralization creates challenges of coordination and control. Both sets of leaders struggle to develop appropriate information and reporting systems, agonize over the right balance between providing incentives and exercising control, and work hard to reinforce the organization's central mission and culture in far-flung and disparate units.

Industry and academe both pay a price for decentralization. For example, such structuring may lead an organization to be more vulnerable to the occasional ethical lapse, financial surprise, or public-relations debacle.

Labor Constraints

Industry managers have traditionally complained that labor unions restrict their flexibility to change operational methods, reassign employees, alter incentive compensation plans, and augment or reduce the labor force. While these laments are diminishing as organized labor's influence in American wanes, in some countries—notably Germany and, to a lesser extent, Japan—these constraints quite powerfully restrict an employer's freedom to manage the workforce.

Unions exist in academe as well. Faculties, staffs, and even graduate students are often organized, if only informally. Academic administrators can easily end up in the same confrontational battles as their industrial management counterparts.

The academy has one additional significant labor constraint: faculty tenure. As most corporate executives would prefer to operate in a nonunion environment, I suspect most academic leaders would not invent tenure if they were designing a higher education system from scratch.

The long probationary period for faculty—typically seven years—combined with the gravity of the decision to grant tenure (are faculty peers prepared to embrace the candidate as a colleague for thirty to forty years?) are powerful quality control mechanisms that are not apparent to critics who focus solely on tenure's lifetime employment guarantee.

Compare this situation with the difficulty that many industrial managers have in parting company with the mediocre but adequate employee who stays on year after year. In large corporations that are fiscally stable, employees often may achieve de facto tenure. They face little risk of dismissal, short of the entire enterprise falling. Moreover, in our age of widespread litigation, employees in all organizations in this country have a heavy arsenal of legal weapons (e.g., alleging discrimination, wrongful termination, etc.) to help them keep their jobs.

A loose comparison can also be made between the "golden parachute" policies established to protect industry's senior executives (and some academic CEOs as well) and tenure. Both evolved to address the same issue: fear of abrupt and capricious dismissal.

The "Not Invented Here" Syndrome

A common shortcoming of both business and academic organizations has been the dismissal of all ideas and practices not "invented" within the enterprise. But such myopia is on the wane. Japanese industrial managers have demonstrated to their global counterparts the benefits of learning from others. The trend toward benchmarking—methodically seeking out best practices in other organizations, then documenting and emulating them—is mushrooming. At the same time, companies have recognized the value of building alliances and joint ventures with partners. Such team building, both domestic and international, effectively shares talent and resources across enterprises. Often the key benefit is organizational learning.

Higher education is following industry's lead. Benchmarking in the academy has focused primarily on administrative areas, but a recent broadening to include educational outcomes assessment is likely to accelerate the benchmarking of teaching and learning processes as well. Colleges and universities are discovering that they have a great deal to learn from other institutions of all types, not solely the academic "elites."

Some of today's most innovative approaches to teaching and learning are in fact emerging from institutions that do not appear on anyone's "top-ten" list.

Higher education is also reaping the benefits of increased cooperation among schools. For example, even the wealthiest colleges and universities now share library resources. Consortia across the nation, from the cluster of Connecticut River Valley colleges in western Massachusetts to my own multi-college community of Claremont, have learned to share a host of class offerings, specialized student services, and selected administrative functions. Financial pressure—a reality now for virtually all colleges and universities—is great medicine for the "not invented here" syndrome.

The Recruitment Process

The academic hiring process, for both faculty and administrators, often appears inefficient in the extreme. Colleges and universities form multi-constituency task forces, search far and wide, and consume months of time and effort in hiring a faculty member or senior-level administrator. Presidential search committees are especially thorough and consult with a wide range of constituencies. Without defending the whole cumbersome process, I will point out that industry is adopting some useful aspects of it. Note how broad and lengthy key industrial searches have become, how often candidates are subjected to a great number of individual interviews by both senior and peer members of the organization, and the important role that those peer evaluations play in the final hiring decision.

Leading Versus Managing

Management literature and development programs stress that presidents must lead, not just manage. As business educator Warren Bennis observes:

> In contrast to just "good managers," true leaders . . . affect the culture, are the social architects of their organizations and create and maintain values. . . . The standard criteria for choosing top-level managers are technical competence, people skills,

conceptual skills, judgment and character. And yet effective leadership is overwhelmingly the function of only one of these: character.[3]

If industry has led academe in implementing many changes in practices and behaviors, leadership is one area where the academy has been out in front—and for good reason. Successful academic presidents have led the way in emphasizing leadership over management for two reasons. First, they are required to deal with—because they are in a very real sense dependent upon—a broad assortment of constituencies. Second, they couldn't manage most of these constituencies if they wished! The constituencies include faculty, students, alumni, donors, legislators, the public, trustees, and administrative staffs. The college or university president can manage only the last of these in a classic command-and-control sense. The rest can, and often actually do, thumb their noses at directives. They must be led, inspired, coaxed, encouraged, cajoled, supported, and coached instead.

As industry begins to recognize the organizational payoffs that come from being responsive to a multitude of constituencies (e.g., customers, suppliers, employees, directors, the community, joint venture and alliance partners) and delegating authority and responsibility to empowered employees, it too is placing new emphasis on the chief executive's responsibility to lead as well as manage.

While academic executives may have pioneered the art of leading constituencies, on some dimensions industrial chiefs have been quicker to recognize the need to focus their leadership skills on shifting organizational cultures to fit new competitive, financial, and technological realities. Furthermore, their leadership has produced higher rates of change. This difference becomes most evident when one compares the most prestigious institutions in the two realms. The top industrial companies have aggressively sought to adapt their corporate cultures to changing conditions; in contrast, the most elite academic institutions have been among the least adaptive.

The preceding catalog of challenges and responses shared by industry and academe is not meant to be exhaustive. Other potential challenges the two worlds may share, or soon share, include downsizing

---

[3] An Invented Life, Addison-Wesley, 1993, pp. 75–78.

their organizations, struggling to turn fixed expenses into variable expenses, engaging in image management, and modernizing the management of their financial and physical assets.

PERSISTENT DIFFERENCES

Despite the many parallels, certain profound and entrenched differences must be respected when industry and the academy consider adopting each other's organizational and management models. Some of these differences lie in the following areas:

- market definition
- quality assessment
- outcomes measurement
- accreditation
- academic freedom
- resistance to change
- market fragmentation
- capital markets

Market Definition

The customer set in higher education is somewhat unclear. Unlike industry where customer and product are two distinct entities, in academe students are a primary customer on the one hand and on the other, they are the "raw material" that higher education processes into output, or product. In business the key customer is the person or entity that pays for the service or product; in education this is not necessarily so. Higher education administrators view faculty and donors, as well as students, as important customers; for the public colleges and universities this list expands to include elected representatives. The rules of supply and demand are different as well. Selective academic institutions that experience excessive demand generally refuse to expand supply (i.e., service more student-customers). They are most unlikely to add capacity to accommodate more students.

Quality Assessment

While in industry the chief arbiters of quality are clearly the customers, faculty define quality in higher education. Colleges and universities are, however, gradually coming to recognize an increasing need to focus on quality feedback from their various constituencies.

Outcomes Measurement

Industry's imperative to focus on profit maximization may put excessive emphasis on short-term, bottom-line results, but it does provide a convenient and fundamental measure of success. Academe, on the other hand, continues to struggle with appropriate ways to measure its outcomes. How should the quality of education be determined? Should standardized tests be used to measure learning? Are job placements a reasonable outcome measure if most institutions consider themselves in the business of educating students for life rather than for specific jobs? How can the more subtle purposes of higher education—e.g., developing responsible citizens and acquainting students with their own and other cultures—be measured systematically?

Traditional measures of academic quality focus largely on inputs (e.g., number of faculty, class size, library volumes). In the absence of reliable and clear outcome measures, colleges and universities tend to organize and conduct their affairs with an eye to satisfying the faculty. Put another way, in the absence of clearly defined external objectives, faculties will adopt objectives that are particularly to their benefit.

Accreditation

Peer review is the essence of higher education's accreditation process. Accreditation, nominally voluntary in academe, is deemed necessary because of higher education's public service responsibilities. While regulation of industry may be roughly parallel to accreditation and virtually all professions are licensed by panels consisting of peers, academic accreditation is far more pervasive—and, unfortunately, often more political.

Academic Freedom

The principle of academic freedom, preserved in higher education by constitution and culture, has no counterpart in industry. One by-product of academic freedom is frequent, open, and vociferous criticism of management, particularly by faculty and students. Increasingly, these attacks lack civility and consideration of other viewpoints. (Similar contentiousness can arise in industry when labor unions are strong and labor-management communications break down, but it represents the exceptional case.) Ultimately, the exercise of academic freedom in some cases may breed a form of political correctness that inhibits rather than promotes freedom of expression.

Resistance to Change

While resistance to change is hardly absent from industrial organizations, it is far more rampant on college and university campuses. This is due in part to the prevailing academic culture which requires consensus decision making. Conservatism is primarily reinforced by two of the academy's constituent groups: students and alumni. But faculty and many administrators share that conservatism. Their resistance is understandable: they have sought scholarly careers at least in part because such careers are perceived to be secure, stable, predictable, and free of many strict deadlines. For administrators at elite private institutions and, until recently, most public institutions, income stability and the resulting lack of financial pressure have sustained a natural conservatism and a persistent aversion to radical institutional transformation. Thus ironically, while they exhort students to continuously change and improve through learning, academic institutions themselves too seldom practice what they preach.

Academe's struggle to adapt to a changing environment parallels one particular segment of industry: the public utilities. With deregulation the utilities are being plugged into turmoil as they try to adapt to a competitive environment. Managements of these companies are working hard to change their organizational cultures. As higher education prepares for the changes that will be demanded of it over the next several decades, its administrators may discern useful lessons from their utility industry colleagues.

Resistance to change is also reinforced by the important role that tradition plays in the life of an academic institution. Academic presidents must be attentive to institutional traditions. They see themselves as part of those traditions, and their plans for the future must be respectful of both the past and the need to ensure institutional continuity and longevity. By contrast, the industrial chief executive is much less tradition-bound. He or she may welcome the many positive benefits arising from a sharp break from past practices and view a future company merger or acquisition as logical and desirable.

Market Fragmentation

Higher education's market is highly fragmented. There is a great diversity across institutions and within segments of the market (e.g., liberal arts colleges, engineering programs, doctoral programs). Unlike other industries, higher education has no single institution that enjoys a commanding market share, even of a single segment. Moreover, academic institutions are typically not motivated to grow or gain market share in terms of student enrollment (although some will fight to maintain enrollments at optimal levels).

Market fragmentation accounts for why, although individual colleges and universities have changed only slowly and incrementally during the last several decades, the universe of higher education was reshaped dramatically. The sum of incremental changes on many campuses (e.g., growth in total enrollment, increased emphasis on adult students, development of executive programs, satellite campuses and remote delivery, a shift toward career-oriented majors) has resulted in far greater mission diversity among America's approximately 3,000 higher education institutions than was the case during the first half of this century.

Capital Markets

Mergers, takeovers, and leveraged buyouts redistribute capital in industry among winners and losers. The ever-present threat of such actions normally encourages corporate corrective action before a fiscal crisis accelerates. No similar capital market operates in academe (although the occasional institutional merger does occur). Well-endowed academic institutions are particularly shielded from fiscal threats. Furthermore, because industrial concerns have access to well-organized capital markets for both equity and debt, they can alter their capital structures to implement a revised strategy much more rapidly than can their academic counterparts.

LESSON TO BE LEARNED

The widespread view that industry and the academy are worlds apart and subject to very different external forces is incorrect. Not only are these institutions more similar than popularly depicted, their similarities are growing, not diminishing. In many ways they address challenges and opportunities with the same management methods and behaviors.

When business executives assume roles as members of higher education governing boards, and conversely, when educators join corporate boards, they need not and should not assume that their career experiences are irrelevant to their new roles—quite the opposite is the case.

Senior academic administrators would do well to devote more time to understanding management and leadership practices in industry and considering how they apply, perhaps with modification, to their academic institutions. Some critics are prone to paraphrase Henry Higgins in *My Fair Lady* in decrying, "Why can't universities and colleges be run more like businesses?" My response: "They can be and they are." We need to remain sensitive to the distinct differences between the academy and industry—in mission, in constituencies, in measurement of outcomes—but the similarities and thus the lessons available from across the gulf that has existed for too long between the academy and industry deserve at least as much attention.

Perhaps most importantly, the very fact that the academy and industry are similar and growing more alike presents some interesting challenges and learning opportunities for leaders in both realms.

Let me suggest a sobering fact for leaders in both camps. I can think of no revolutionary new product or service that has spawned an entire new industry which emanated from an institution with a major position in a related existing market. Nor do any dominant suppliers to existing related markets come to mind. Examples run the gamut from mini-computers to personal software to overnight package delivery to airport hotels to microwave ovens to distance learning. Notable innovators in the academic arena are two for-profit corporations: DeVry Institute and the University of Phoenix. The economist Joseph Schumpeter's classic principle of creative destruction seems to be alive and well. Innovative entrepreneurs will over time bring down existing market leaders, the destruction often driven by technology, one of the key external forces identified earlier. As new opportunities emerge in industry and higher education (e.g., teaching in fundamentally different ways to different students at different stages in their lives), will our major institutions prove to be more adaptable in the future than they have been in the past?

Leaders in the two realms have for too long ignored each other, certain that their different environments demand very different management behaviors. Each has tended to drift into a certain self-satisfaction, even smugness, in the view that little can be learned from the other. The time is overdue to recognize that the differences have sharply diminished, and thus both for-profit and academic leaders have much to learn from their opposite numbers.

Chapter 2

::

Leveraged Learning:

Technology's Role in Restructuring Higher Education

Sally V. Massy, **Jackson Hole Higher Education Group**

::

Higher education faces many challenges as the twenty-first century approaches. Public and private dollars are being siphoned off to other social concerns, consumers are balking at rising tuition rates, and critics are questioning academic productivity and the quality of undergraduate programs. Many colleges and universities are pushing the limits of their budgets, personnel, and facilities to serve a broader population of students whose goals, preparations, and preferred modes of attendance are more diverse than ever before. Resources are further strained as institutions try to cope with today's unprecedented information explosion. And looming ominously on the horizon are external competitors who threaten to break traditional higher education's near monopoly by offering attractive, cost-effective learning alternatives.

Academe's conventional response to crisis—to raise tuitions and trim costs—is impractical given today's constrained environment. In any case, higher education's current problems cannot be solved by money alone. A new set of attitudes and behaviors is required. Significantly, a fresh response to crisis is gaining ground: the fundamental restructuring of colleges and universities. How will such restructuring improve quality, reduce costs, and enhance productivity? Who should lead the effort and what should it entail? Our roundtable conversation revealed a considerable difference of opinion on these issues. But the panel did agree that any successful transformation—the kind that will enable an institution to survive and prosper into the next century—must include the effective and intelligent use of information technology.

DEGREES OF CHANGE

Our roundtable began with two presentations, one on restructuring and another on technology. These talks stimulated a subsequent wide-ranging discussion of what should constitute academic change in higher education and how technology could be used to achieve such change. Discussants were cautious or optimistic depending on how strongly change-related threats or opportunities were perceived in their own professional lives. Those working outside the academy tended to be daring and visionary. Their call for the radical reengineering of higher education stemmed from a firsthand knowledge of the rewards of process redesign. Having witnessed the substantial strides made by business and other societal sectors in responding to environmental change, they were clearly disconcerted by the lack of similar movement in higher education.

The outsiders challenged academy members to examine higher education's organizational structures for signs of obsolescence. They suggested that old frames of reference be discarded if they locked educators into traditional but anachronistic behaviors—thinking in terms of "courses and instructors," for example, rather than "modules and competencies." They urged higher education to shift paradigms and use students instead of faculty as the basic blocks of organizational design on which the academic infrastructure rests. Colleges and universities should become learner-centered, they argued, especially now that technology empowers them to do so.

The discussion reminded one policy leader of recent encounters with government officials who increasingly spoke of "buying instruction, not faculty"—implying that if attractive alternatives were available, the government was not wedded to traditional faculty-centered education across the board.

"Unfortunately," lamented a second leader, "institutional administrators often are wedded to existing structures and will fight to keep them even if it means reducing enrollments and turning down qualified students, as it has in California's financially stricken state university system." Another participant observed that institutional desire to maintain the status quo and the almost categorical imperative that faculty seem to have about replicating themselves make it especially difficult to fund significant change. "We are in the business of 'maximizing monks' "—providing colleagues and ensuring "the persistence of the faith," as it were. Accordingly, "we have pre-sold our revenue stream in faculty compensation. That's why we don't have the money for implementing change. We need to transform the transactional base of the enterprise."

Discussants who were or had been academic administrators acknowledged academe's structural conservatism but expressed their own enthusiasm for change. "This system can't survive in its current state," remarked one, noting that rising student enrollments at public institutions and burgeoning amounts of new knowledge to be archived were already testing the fiscal and spatial limits of many colleges and universities under the present system.

Other administrators, their visions tempered by a pragmatism borne from years of negotiating through flat hierarchies and diffuse authority, agreed change was necessary but favored a less radical approach. Aggressive incrementalism—"continuously improving what we do today"—would avoid full-scale revolt among their constituents and result in less disruptive long-term positive change.

A few roundtable participants, mostly faculty, felt that minimal change was warranted. To them, American higher education was not "broken" and therefore did not need to be "fixed." Don't understate the success of American education," one admonished. "It is not an industry that is about to die."

For the majority who felt change to higher education's academic culture was imperative whether through gradual continuous quality improvements, radical process reengineering, or a managed hybrid of the two, a key question was whether reforms should simply reshape and expand instructional delivery—taking full advantage of the new digital technologies available—or whether they should overhaul the basic content and structure of curricula. Advocates for the latter position felt that higher education was suffering from "curriculum sprawl" caused by years of lax control over faculty pursuits. Fewer offerings more tightly focused, they felt, would lead to greater cohesion and cost-effectiveness.

But others wondered if economic pressures and course standardization would lead to the homogenization of instruction. "If we offer only 'the best of this' and 'the best of that,' one former administrator reflected, might it not lead to an unfortunate shallowing of diversity?" Several participants responded by expressing their belief that, in the future, institutions might in fact be able to offer a greater selection of subject matter cogently and cost-effectively by leveraging instruction with technology.

TECHNOLOGY'S ROLE IN ACADEMIC RESTRUCTURING

Information technology was identified as an invaluable tool that could bring a much needed elasticity to academe's historically rigid structures. Replacing cumbersome and out-moded academic processes with new technological approaches enables institutions to manage information flow more efficiently and respond to heightened market demands for responsiveness, convenience, and flexibility. Like football quarterbacks calling audibles at the line, institutions that apply technology throughout their academic core will be able to adjust to unfolding developments in a timely and effective manner. Costly inefficiencies in academic planning can be located and eliminated, large volumes of data can be collected to establish benchmarks of "best practice," and the vertically organized structure of the academy—with its "silos" of isolated departments and hierarchies—can be transformed into a horizontal, networked structure that facilitates group problem solving and cooperative knowledge exchange across disciplines.

As imperative as it is that technology be incorporated into academic processes, however, roundtable participants warned educators not to respond blindly to its siren call. Technology's mere availability should not be cause alone to restructure. Rather, institutional threats and opportunities should drive change. The key, the group emphasized, is to regard technology as a powerful tool that can be dynamically and creatively applied to challenges ahead. To examine technology's impact in this role more closely, the roundtable group broke into three sections focusing on pedagogy, faculty roles, and economics, respectively.

Pedagogy

Participants quickly identified technology's pedagogical advantages. First, they noted, it promotes active learning, fully engaging students in their education. The new tools of technology enable students to be masters of an interactive universe of ideas rather than passive receptacles of knowledge. Aided by powerful computers, students can tackle complex real-world applications and sophisticated simulations instead of watered-down textbook problem sets unrelated to life after college.

Participants believed that technology's greatest impact on instruction would fall in the area of so-called codified knowledge—the transmission of facts, theories, and the development of cognitive skills. Some felt that technology could well play a primary educating role in this regard, enabling students to learn certain concepts independently of place or time. One participant reported a research finding that at least 67% of existing instructional material could be effectively presented on CD-ROM for this purpose. Critical when developing this type of instructional technology, the group emphasized, is for educators to ensure it enhances a student's set of learning tools and isn't simply used to "replace lecturers on stage by talking heads on video."

Another pedagogical advantage is that students are no longer intellectually limited to the confines of their campus. Given a robust campus infrastructure that provides quick and convenient access to a rich diversity of network resources, students can seek out knowledge at the frontiers in addition to (or in place of) "canned" wisdom they receive from instructors in lecture form.

Technology also promotes cooperative learning. The group thought that the computer's usefulness as a communications facilitator might in fact exceed its value as an instructional device. Not only do computer networks facilitate collaboration among students (and faculty) on campus, they enable students to communicate directly with experts off-site and participate in research projects around the world. Networks also provide students with opportunities to distribute their intellectual work products globally for a level of feedback potentially far greater than could ever be achieved in class.

Technology's ability to tailor instruction to individual learning styles and pace was also noted. The mass customization of higher education is no longer outside the realm of possibility. Technology can be designed that allows students to learn at a natural and appropriate level for their ability rather than being artificially constrained by the level of other learners in the classroom or even by the nominal level of their institution. Indeed, given a ubiquitous educational computing network, the borders between high school, college, and adult education will grow less distinct as students grow accustomed to traveling back and forth electronically across them.

The question was then posed: If higher learning becomes conveniently and ubiquitously accessible through electronic means, what value will traditional colleges and universities have? A veteran professor responded immediately. "Our institutions will continue to offer two elements that are vital to a satisfying learning experience—structure and certification." His research showed that students fare best in programs that define intermediate milestones, monitor and record progress, and provide assessment and formal recognition of accomplishments. Students also benefit from a system of accreditation that validates their accomplishments for an outside world. Colleges and universities have a long-established track record of competently providing these essential services, he noted.

Asked if it wouldn't be possible to provide structure and certification outside of the university system, several participants pointed to traditional higher education's other, exclusive advantages. The dynamic characteristics of a live classroom cannot be digitally duplicated. Classroom students capture rich contextual cues and learn appropriate academic behaviors by observing instructors and fellow classmates. They enjoy the spontaneity of real-time interactions. Electronic instruction lacks the human "electricity" that an enthusiastic professor sends through an audience. The praises and prods of a respected live instructor compel students more than the synthetic "sticks" and "carrots" of a computer.

The socialization benefits of a traditional campus-based education were also noted. Participants felt that many graduating high school seniors and their parents would continue to value college as a rite of passage that molds comportment and smoothes the transition into adult life. Beyond developing intellectual skills, a well-structured undergraduate experience can enhance a person's "emotional intelligence"—the set of social skills that some researchers have deemed as significant as conventional intelligence to future success.

Participants believed that education delivered exclusively through electronic means would most appeal to adult learners seeking specific codified knowledge and certification. These students are frequently constrained in time and place by personal and work-related responsibilities and are generally seeking to advance themselves professionally more than socially. It was acknowledged, however, that students in all market segments would likely appreciate some opportunity to leverage their time and educational dollars by using technology in lieu of more traditional learning methods.

While many colleges and universities are actively weaving technology into their work, institutions that traditionally emphasize undergraduate education over research—e.g., liberal arts and community colleges—appear most dedicated to integrating technology specifically into instruction. Representatives from this sector suggested that perhaps collaborations would develop between their schools and large research universities that typically spend significant tuition revenue on financing faculty research but feel pressure now to redirect funds and attention to undergraduate education. Rather than reinventing the wheel, these universities might tap into the considerable instruction and technology expertise that the colleges have developed in exchange for offering access to other resources and expertise that they, the universities, control.

Overall, participants believed that the convenience and flexibility technology offers, combined with its potential to reduce costs and improve educational quality, guarantee its broader penetration of teaching and learning processes in the future.

Faculty Roles

Participants in this breakout group concluded that if indeed a new teaching and learning environment emerges as a result of several factors including technology, faculty roles will be reshaped. Many envisioned a new system that is learner-centered and structured around educational goals instead of discipline-based curricula. Competency "modules" and progress "gates" might compete with or replace courses and grades as the basic units of academic accounting. Sophisticated computer databases and networking would facilitate the precise tracking of student progress and preference needed for such an enterprise.

For such a restructured academy to succeed, faculty would need to enhance certain existing skills and master new ones. Chief among their new functions would be acting as design engineers. Faculty would be tasked with crafting coherent academic programs from a universe of complex and wide-ranging choices. Such programs would offer a variety of clear goals to appeal to a diverse student population. Presently, few faculty take the time to think systematically this way; most focus only on the development and delivery of the courses they are assigned to teach. In the future, faculty will be compelled to take a more global approach to learning. They will spend less time preparing and "professing" theories and facts and more time managing the process of education, inside the classroom and out. Trained "para-faculty" and a variety of instructional technologies will leverage faculty time, freeing professors to devote more time to tasks where they can provide greater comparative value.

Faculty must learn to integrate appropriate technologies intelligently into learning processes as part of their educational design and management duties. They must understand and adopt different approaches for different domains. Students seeking specific content and competency in, for example, composition, language acquisition, and vocational studies might well be served by computer-based simulations and other courseware. Other students seeking broader knowledge—"what the educated person ought to know"—might focus on building a set of general computing and communication skills that can be used throughout a lifetime of learning. The ability to successfully navigate global information networks is an example of one such skill.

Future faculty might also play a role analogous to health care's primary-care physicians. Assigned a group of students to monitor, a faculty member would periodically review performance portfolios, advise and consult, and manage student "hand-offs" to relevant faculty specialists. Much of this activity could be done on-line. Ideally in this paradigm, the "primary-care" faculty member would identify student difficulties as they emerged and intervene promptly with appropriate remediation. Diagnoses could be informed by reports automatically generated from instructional technologies.

Participants predicted that the faculty's prime role inside the classroom would shift from that of deliverer of theory and facts to modeler of competence. A faculty member's comparative advantage is in his or her ability to convey non-codifiable knowledge: describing context and relevance, helping students interpret what they are learning, and demonstrating from personal experience how a practitioner approaches the challenges in his or her discipline—in short, acting in the role of master to apprentice. Computers cannot adequately substitute for humans here, they can only facilitate the transmission of this sort of knowledge. If technology is used to deliver an appropriate portion of a course's essential codified material, faculty will be freed to spend a greater portion of their time communicating non-codifiable knowledge. And students, primed by computer in the basic theories and facts, might enjoy, along with the faculty, the prospects of starting class discussions on a deeper initial plane.

Faculty will continue their role as content experts. However, because of the boom in knowledge generation, they will necessarily be true experts on smaller and smaller slices of the knowledge pie. Some will be threatened by this loss of control and the fact that their students may have access to cutting-edge information on-line as quickly as they do. It will become harder to retain the "Wizard of Oz" image of an all-knowing, all-being professor if students can easily "pull back the curtain," as it were, by efficiently gathering opinions and knowledge from sources around the world that might contradict or supersede the professor's. The trick for faculty is to shed this persona voluntarily and turn the changed circumstances to their advantage. Participants thought that, in the future, faculty and students would more often share the adventure of seeking new knowledge together. Emphasis will shift from developing an encyclopedic mastery of one's field to honing skills that enable sought-after knowledge to be obtained "just in time," navigating quickly to areas both on-line and off that will supplement one's existing knowledge base appropriately.

Increasing numbers of faculty will use their status as content experts to enter into partnerships with nonprofit and commercial developers of courseware and other educational software products. It was conceded that commercial developers with their ready access to capital, marketing expertise, and human resources are probably more effective than academic institutions in managing these projects successfully. One member made an analogous reference to the way computer operating systems evolved in academe. In the old days, institutions had to custom-build their own. They were idiosyncratic and not easily adaptable to other machines or institutions. In-house development burned valuable resources at a healthy clip. Now off-the-shelf operating systems are used almost exclusively at colleges and universities. Applications software is also purchased from third parties but often comes with software "hooks" that allow for end-user customization. The participants envisioned academe's role in educational software development taking a similar course. Alternatively in certain cases, projects might originate at universities but then spin off into separate corporate entities, à la Netscape, after reaching a critical mass.

Faculty will also need to become better at collaborating with their peers, both on-campus and off. They will need to break out of their isolated shells and departmental silos to facilitate cooperative learning and reap the advantages of sharing resources.

Institutions cannot expect faculty to pick up these new skills entirely on their own. For faculty to succeed in their new roles, institutions will need to provide adequate training and support. One discussant reported that currently only about 30 percent of college campuses have formal teaching and learning centers. More will need to be established to enhance faculty skills, especially in innovative areas such as interactive instruction, sharing resources electronically, and matching technologies to educational domains.

Over the long run, the breakout group felt that efforts will need to focus on the point at which faculty enter the "pipeline"—i.e., graduate education. The pipeline needs to be fixed. It is at this critical point in a future professor's career, before habits are locked in, that pedagogical training can make the greatest impact. Graduate students arguably also have more time and energy to devote to exploring innovative teaching approaches. In their role as mentors and modelers of appropriate academic behaviors, faculty must signal that teaching is held in the same high regard as research and that honing this skill is worthwhile. The group suggested that more apprentice teaching programs be developed and that teaching advisory centers design programs that specifically appeal to this audience.

Economics

Participants were fairly optimistic that technology would offer many opportunities to revamp cost structures and gain efficiencies without sacrificing educational quality. In some cases technology might in fact improve quality while reducing costs.

Libraries, for example, can likely reduce their costs, in terms of both dollars and space, and improve quality by archiving certain materials digitally. Reference volumes and technical journals are especially good candidates for such storage—neither are particularly valued as artifacts and both have relatively short shelf lives. In physical form they are costly to acquire and use up valuable shelf space. Conversely, their digital forms take up little space, are less fragile, and most importantly, enhance educational utility. Electronic texts can be searched and sorted quickly and flexibly. Information "comes alive" in electronic journals as readers manipulate animated conceptual models, download data into spreadsheets for further evaluation, and double-click on words and phrases to reveal related hypertext descriptions.

One member of the group observed that intelligent applications of technology can transform higher education from essentially a labor-intensive "handicraft" industry to a more capital-intensive endeavor where productivity increases are easier to achieve and expected on a regular basis. This happens by altering the labor-capital mix for teaching and learning. Pressure to pursue this option will grow unless per-student budgets increase dramatically and, while new investments will have to come at the expense of some labor inputs—including faculty positions— several in the group felt the proposal was not altogether a bad idea. Conventional processes in higher education require extensive investments in office, classroom, and laboratory space and support—more than may be required when technology is effectively deployed for similar purposes. Changing the labor/capital mix by leveraging critical faculty labor and facilities with appropriate technology enables long-term productivity improvements because the per-unit cost of technology is dropping in real terms while those of faculty and facilities continue to rise. The group was adamant, however, that faculty will continue to be critical to a quality education and that what was being considered was intelligent leveraging, not wholesale replacement.

One participant offered a good example of such leveraging: the case of Rensselaer Polytechnic Institute. A few years ago, RPI was faced with a significant structural deficit and a high first-year dropout rate. In response, they set aggressive restructuring goals and specific financial targets to get back on track. Notable among faculty efforts was the introduction of a set of math and science courses that used an innovative "studio" approach to learning. The program combines lecture, review, and laboratory work in one setting and uses technology extensively. Students are presented with a rich interactive environment that most favor over more conventional formats. RPI found that, since the innovatively structured studio courses take less faculty time than separate lecture, review, and lab sessions, over the long run they cost less.

A roundtable member from outside the academy stressed the importance of setting specific targets, as RPI did, for achieving actual change and not just continuing to talk about it. It had been his observation that too often academic institutions were not disciplined in this way. "Frankly," he added, "members of the corporate world are sometimes amazed at the diffuse authority and lack of firm targets or commitments they find on campuses. This instills little of the confidence a commercial developer needs in order to invest in bringing major new educational products to market. Higher education can be fickle and trendy in its desires, yet developers need significant lead times to develop suitable products. Software suppliers can be most responsive to higher education's needs," he said, "when they clearly understand what should be provided and at what price."

Popular and efficient courseware enables institutions to achieve significant economies of scale, delivering education to large numbers of students at low marginal cost. Reluctance to adopt courseware "not invented here"—even when developers offer to train faculty in its use—has limited many institutions from achieving such economics. Marketing is also often directed at the wrong targets within an institution, i.e., those without curricular or purchase authority.

"Perhaps, we can take a lesson from developments in the commercial aviation industry," another participant suggested. Aircraft manufacturers routinely work together with clients to develop the performance and cost specifications for each generation of airplanes. By ensuring a minimum level of demand for a product before it goes into production, the partnership encourages innovation and holds down end-user costs by removing risk premiums from pricing.

One participant floated the idea that possibly a major institutional consortium—with experience in working together on other matters—might collaborate on developing courseware specifications for one or more introductory courses that traditionally draw high enrollments. A second discussant suggested that the individual members of such a consortium pledge small percentages of their undergraduate teaching budgets as a firm sign of commitment.

Some felt that perhaps entities external to the academy would provide all the resources for development, but the majority felt that colleges and universities could not depend on others to do their work for them. The effort must come from within. Funding for technology infrastructure should be integrated formally into operating budgets. "We have to stop funding IT projects with 'budget dust'," one participant wryly noted. It is fine to be opportunistic, but budgetary planning must come from the top down as well as the bottom up.

The roundtable group singled out the establishment of a robust computing and communications infrastructure as another important key to leveraging educational resources. Networking extends the institution, bringing the world to the campus and the campus to the world. It makes for a highly cost-effective channel of distribution. The power of all connected colleges and universities combine to form a virtual "mega-university" whose resources can be tapped inexpensively and powerfully.

Increasingly, the cost of devices that plug into the network will be carried by individual users as such devices become more affordable and portable. Institutions will be able to concentrate their investments on improving existing infrastructure—e.g., supplying high-bandwidth networking, high-speed ports and convenient wireless connections, and peripherals such as large screen monitors, scanners, printers and mass storage units.

Institutions that neglect technology will run the risk in the future of being marginalized in favor of educational systems that more effectively serve a generation of learners accustomed to the benefits of ubiquitous computing and communication. Some participants were concerned that educators were ignoring the potential of external competition in higher education's future. Many still think of higher education in terms of a closed market. But as information becomes more fluid and easily exchanged, higher education's barriers to entry are falling. A massive physical infrastructure for learning is no longer necessary to appeal to some expanding market segments.

Outsiders will use information technology as a lever to pry open a market that heretofore has been the exclusive domain of colleges and universities. In the past, distance learning programs have been offered, but they have been distinctly different from campus-based learning. With advances in technology on campus, these differences are blurring. Some learners will choose these alternatives immediately, perhaps not happily at first but driven of necessity. As momentum builds and a critical mass of learners experience positive educational results, acceptance will accelerate. One professor remarked that members of the academy seem little concerned with this possibility—or perhaps they are unaware of it. "Ironically," he said, "the same faculty members who are fighting now against any substitution of information technology for their labors may find themselves blindsided down the road by a much greater force that simply eliminates their institution altogether."

On the other hand, it was agreed that, with adequate planning, many vulnerable institutions could survive by using the new technologies to their own advantage—tailoring instruction to the individual, allocating resources more precisely, expanding their own markets beyond traditional geographic boundaries, and collaborating with other educational institutions and commercial providers to develop joint programs and share costly resources and expertise. Increasing pressures to compete might also lead colleges and universities to critically evaluate their institutional identity and sharpen their comparative advantage for more effective strategic positioning.

IMPEDIMENTS TO CHANGE

So if information technology holds such great potential for higher education, why hasn't it penetrated the academic core more completely already? To be sure, it has revolutionized the way scholars do research. And it is dramatically reshaping the way administrative tasks are performed. But why hasn't it more profoundly impacted what is arguably higher education's most critical mission? Why hasn't the teaching and learning process been infused with technology on a broader scale?

"It's rational resistance for the most part," observed one member with broad experience in applying technology to learning. "The technology has been difficult to use. The incentives will be there when it is simpler."

"More training and support would help," suggested another. A third discussant's remarks clearly resonated with the group: "Most of all, we need time to take advantage of the training and support."

Indeed it surfaced that academe is plagued with an institutional form of attention deficit disorder. Faculty members do not have sufficient time to do everything well that is demanded of them. Consequently, they set expedient priorities and continually thrash between one duty and another. They are left feeling fragmented and frustrated.

The condition has become more acute as the rate at which information is generated has exploded. Information is the raw material that faculty use to shape new knowledge. And as Nobel Laurete Herbert Simon noted recently in Scientific American, "what information consumes is obvious. It consumes the attention of its recipients." Simon draws the logical conclusion that "a wealth of information creates a poverty of attention." It also creates "a need to allocate the attention efficiently among the overabundance of information sources that might consume it." (*Scientific American*, September 1995, p. 201)

Roundtable participants felt that many faculty members—particularly those at research universities—make little effort to incorporate technology into their instruction for the same reason they push teaching to the bottom of their priorities: they are trying to optimize the allocation of their attention. Since existing incentives and rewards favor research activities and prestigious national service, given a finite amount of time, the professors concentrate on these pursuits.

One participant noted that faculty generally do manage to acquire and learn technologies that enhance their research. "Unsurprising," he said, "considering that tangible rewards for a job well done and painful consequences for a poor performance are handed out in this arena." The research process is consistently monitored by peers. The teaching process, on the other hand, is left largely unmonitored. Instruction goes on quietly "behind closed doors." Another participant likened the teaching process to a rental car. No one owns it and therefore no one is overly concerned with the way it gets treated. Only gross and overt abuse draws action; otherwise there is little accountability.

The mention of accountability elicited a warning from a discussant whose research showed that faculty also avoid technology because they fear it might facilitate an oppressive form of accountability, what the discussant called "measured outcomeness." Faculty find this scenario more frightening than the possibility that technology might somehow dehumanize the academy into a sterile body of "techno-nerds." "To mitigate the faculty's concern," he said, "we must shift assessment away from accountability and toward quality. We need to set up feedback loops that bring a sense of heightened responsibility to the faculty about their role as teachers." A veteran administrator agreed, saying that in his experience an institution "can realign its incentives but after a few years you hit the wall. We have to change paradigms and see faculty as part of the solution; move from inspection assessment to quality improvement."

There was a difference of opinion about how such an effort might get started. Reengineering efforts often fail, it was noted, because there is a lack of commitment at the top. "Presidential leadership is key to getting faculty on board," asserted one faculty member. Another countered, "To wait for presidents...it's going to be a long wait. It's the department that is key. We need to look at the department's core behavior, its internal decision making processes." Restructuring initiatives will necessarily flounder when faculty are more committed to the institution's perimeter than to its core. Feedback loops placed at the departmental level are likely to be the most effective. Today's "hollowed collegiality" needs to be replaced with real collegiality, where faculty on departmental work teams collaborate to set collective goals and where peer pressure is used to bring individual faculty members back in line when their personal goals threaten to grossly supersede institutional ones.

"In my opinion," volunteered one university administrator, "we're also grossly overadministered and by stripping administration away, we will necessarily empower people." He noted that work such as student advising has gravitated to staff members and needs to be taken back by members of the academy.

But a research university professor observed that many of his colleagues were "not going to want to change unless it's 'free' "—in other words, unless their current allocations of discretionary time are left largely undisturbed. Faculty would be unwilling to sacrifice significant amounts of research time to work on institutional initiatives and, he felt, any tinkering with existing rewards and incentives to reshape behavior would prove unpopular. Another participant supported this claim, pointing out that over time faculty have gravitated to the research-oriented "perimeter" of the institution, away from its educational "core." The majority of faculty work in relative isolation and are driven by their own goals, not those of the institution. They feel a sense of entitlement about their chosen pursuits and reject any notion of faculty productivity defined by forces external to their discipline.

Other obstacles to progress were mentioned, including the lack of convenient legal access to intellectual property and copyright clearances and security issues. The leader of one of the breakout sections declared that during their conversation "we weren't worried that teachers were going to be put out of work because of this [technology]." In fact, as another participant pointed out, a market still needs to develop for the products of instructional technology as well as expertise on how to use it. The current market for courseware indeed is "problematic," said a corporate participant, and needs to be subsidized—not just to spur initial development but, even more significantly, to maintain established software through multiple generations as new hardware obsoletes existing versions.

CONCLUSIONS

In the long run, faculty members will have to determine for themselves that changing the educational paradigm is worthwhile. Many of the hurdles encountered when trying to incorporate technology into the teaching and learning process, or when trying to reform academe in general, are organizational, or sociological, rather than technical in nature.

A familiar mantra echoed around the table: "The culture has got to change." The group felt such change would more likely come from crisis than from opportunity. They agreed that institutional leaders are generally loath to suggest substantial policy changes that might give rise to unpleasant politics and campus commotion unless the institution faces an immediate threat to its well-being. The mounting challenges that face higher education are beginning to provide ample impetus. Many colleges and universities that have resisted restructuring and technology in the past are reconsidering their positions. And the stories of successful transformations now emerging may motivate others.

Technology's role in transforming undergraduate education should become a centerpiece of institutional visions and strategic plans. Specific milestones need to be set, responsibilities assigned, budgets allocated, and systems of accountability established. Needed paradigm changes cannot be achieved by uncoordinated individual efforts, although individual initiatives will certainly be essential. The academic department might well become a main agent of change since the actions needed lie beyond the reach of individual professors.

The first necessary step is to affirm or reaffirm the importance of undergraduate education and ensure that teaching commands an appropriate portion of faculty time. Without the dedication of quality time, no exhortations about restructuring or investments in technology can bear fruit. Over time, technology will leverage faculty time, freeing them to pursue the most challenging aspects of teaching, but serious up-front time commitments will be required during the transition. One member of the group, continuing with the clerical metaphor used throughout the roundtable, eloquently summed up what was needed: "We need to build a new church and bring the monks a new theology." Institutions need to make learning the metric, the valued good. They need to harness the work going on at the perimeter and focus on core missions. Undergraduate teaching must emerge from "behind closed doors" to become a collective activity, one which commands the faculty's best attention on both current performance and innovation for future improvements. Only then can the full potential of information technology be realized.

Chapter 3

::

The University of Pennsylvania Health System Model

The Academic Health Center As the Nucleus of an Integrated Health Care Delivery System

William N. Kelley, MD, **University of Pennsylvania**

::

More urgently than in any other part of the university, the academic health center in this era is dealing with the issue of how to balance the requisites of for-profit businesses with the service standards of not-for-profit institutions. The academic health center is at the for-profit/not-for-profit interface, and much of its competition is in the for-profit sector. Therefore, we are obliged to behave more and more like a for-profit company while still protecting all of the virtues and features that are so important to us as an academic institution. The demand to move aggressively to compete with the for-profit sector is so strong that it is going to be a challenge for us and for every academic health center in the country to remember that academic excellence is our true product.

Faculty Recruitment

For me, defending the supremacy of academic excellence means recruiting and retaining the most outstanding people at every level and providing the organization and support needed to help these people be successful. Faculty recruitment truly is our most important job. We make a tremendous effort at every level—be it for a chair, a division chief, a new faculty member, or anybody else—to go out and find for that position one of the top five people in the country. This requires that we have the appropriate currency, which is:

- new or renewed space
- start-up support
- a supportive environment
- incentives to reward individuals for performance

It is interesting that the clinical chairs have supported the implementation of incentives, while the basic science chairs want nothing of them. As a result, we have incentives that relate to recruitment for the clinical chairs and for several others, but we do not have them for the basic science chairs.

The University of Pennsylvania School of Medicine now has some 950 standing faculty or people that are considered regular faculty and another 100 or so research faculty. Altogether this is about 1,050, which is on the small side compared to other top-ten academic health centers. This represents a growth rate of a little over 2 percent since 1989.

There has been a difference between the pattern of growth in the clinical departments and in the basic science departments. We are hovering around 100 faculty in the basic science departments. This number climbed from 90 to 98 in the past year. Twenty years ago, there were 150 faculty in the basic science departments, so that we have shrunken over twenty years while the tremendous growth that occurred was all in the clinical faculty. My expectation is that as time goes on we will see continuation in the growth of the basic science departments, and, maybe, see some decrease in size in the clinical science departments.

We, for many different reasons, have had the unusual opportunity to recruit a large number of chairs. We have 26 departments, and, over the past six years, have recruited 19 new chairs and are, at the moment, actively searching for three additional chairs. Also, the School of Medicine has 16 centers and institutes whose director reports directly to the dean. Of this 16, 11 are new appointments. There has been a great amount of turnover, not by design, but for a variety of different reasons.

It is, of course, difficult to measure the quality of faculty. We have had some small growth in faculty, and I think its quality has continued to improve, although this is very hard to demonstrate based on the numbers that are easily achievable.

Productivity is the best measure. Yet, by the criterion of new memberships in the widely recognized scholarly societies, we appear to be not doing nearly as well as I think we should be doing. We have a total of six from our faculty in the American Philosophical Society and have had two new members elected since 1989. We have ten of our faculty in the American Academy of Arts and Sciences, or which only two have been elected since 1989. We have 13 in the National Academy of Sciences, but only two elected since 1989. We have 18 in the Institute of Medicine with 11 elected since 1989. We have 28 in the Association of American Physicians. However, these academic societies generally require that the individuals be quite senior and distinguished to gain membership. As a measure of productivity, the society that probably means the most to us in terms of membership is the American Society for Clinical Investigation. This organization requires members to be physicians and to be elected before age 45. So, membership really is limited to young physician investigators. In this group, we have had 27 of our 71 faculty members elected since 1989. This is a good measure that some of our young faculty are doing excellent work, since the limit that can be elected nationally is around 60 a year.

We have gone through rather extensive strategic planning, including program planning, education, research, and health-services planning as well as planning for development and fund-raising, overall financial planning, and master site and facilities planning.

Education

Education is one of the three major missions of the University of Pennsylvania School of Medicine. In medicine, for reasons we do not really understand very well, we are experiencing the great good fortune of a tremendous explosion of interest from applicants who wish to go to medical school. Nationally, in the past five years, medical schools have experienced about a 59 percent increase in applicants, despite the fact that there still are only about 16,000 positions for new students. Back in 1989, when this applicant number dropped as low as 27,000 for the 16,000 places, there was a 1.7 or 1.8 ratio of applicants to admissions. This is probably the lowest ratio at which any of us would ever be comfortable. However, right now there are nearly three applicants for every admission nationally.

At Penn we have had the advantage of having an even greater increase, with almost a 90 percent increase in applicants over that same period. The fact is, we can only accept about 400 students to fill a class of 150, and this dramatic increase has really just created more difficulty for us in many ways. However, it does assure that we will have tremendously outstanding students, and that is one benefit that we will nurture in every way we possibly can. We take good care of those students and believe that they are spreading the good word about us—most of the time anyway.

Regardless of its current popularity, we perceive tremendous problems in medical education, as the dramatic changes now occurring in medicine and society clash with resistance to change in medical education. This conflict, in my opinion, is leading rapidly to a serious crisis in medical education. It is unbelievable and truly difficult to understand, but this has been an issue in medicine since 1910. The Flexnor Report of that year was a milestone that documented a change in medicine. However, all the commissions, all the committees, and all the efforts to change medical education since then have effected very little of substance. There have been some minor changes, but virtually none of the recommendations that have come from various national reviews have been taken seriously.

Our view is that we have to address this crisis and create a plan for a medical education process at Penn, which is based on the following:

- The Flexnor Principles, emphasizing the scientific basis of medicine and the need for hands-on clinical learning, must be preserved.
- Physicians must be continuously aware of the new knowledge created by advances in medical research. This requires a commitment to long-term learning.
- Physicians must gain the ability to practice medicine in a cost-constrained environment dominated by managed care in which they will use order sets, critical pathways, and information systems as tools of their practice.
- Physicians must embody the qualities of professionalism and humanism in spite of forces which militate against the development and maintenance of these qualities.
- We must find ways to reduce the cost of medical education in spite of our efforts to improve it.

Our faculty are now considering this challenge of taking these principles and working through them to practicable solutions. We will see what happens. April 1996 marked a milestone event in that we attempted to bring as many faculty members as possible, together with the students, to try to define some really major solutions to the paradox that, despite the tremendous popularity of medical education, we are not teaching students to be physicians in the modern era. This failure has so frustrated some of the HMOs that they have threatened to start their own medical schools.

Research

The University of Pennsylvania School of Medicine has committed itself to implementing a multidisciplinary research program. This is one of the most difficult things for an institution to make succeed. The obvious reason is that the department chairs have a fierce commitment to their own programs. They view anything new that overlays or competes with their programs as not to the benefit of them or their faculty. The key is to develop a process so that potential opponents of the new program will see it as a win-win situation—a win for them and a win for the program. This has been our strategy.

In 1990, our strategic plan for research laid out, foremost, the commitment to multidisciplinary research and, secondly, identified eight special areas where we needed to enhance our commitment. These areas were human gene therapy, retrovirology, the biology of cancer, neuroscience, aging, development biology, structural biology, molecular genetics, and genome mapping. These all are within the biomedical specialties' research area. However, we also wanted to support the multidisciplinary side of health-services research. The strategic plan's vision was used as a blueprint for developing a number of centers called Type 2 Centers, which means that the director reports to the dean, not to the department chair. Over the past five years, we have set up the Institute for Human Gene Therapy; the Center for Bio-Ethics; very recently, the Institute for Medicine and Engineering, which we believe is going to be a great new program; a Center for Experimental Therapeutics; a Center for Sleep; an Institute on Aging; a Center for Clinical Epidemiology and Biostatistics; and a Center for Research on Reproduction and Women's Health. The Center for Research on Reproduction and the Institute on Medicine and Engineering are really just being started, but the others have had a year or two or three to move ahead.

In addition, we have redirected some of the departments. We established a Department of Biostatistics and Epidemiology as a basic science department. We evolved our Department of Anatomy into a new department with a new name, called Cell and Developmental Biology. We have developed two new clinical departments: Emergency Medicine and Family Practice. We have redirected our department of Human Genetics to a Department of Genetics with a much broader mandate to cover nonhuman genetics. We established a Department of Neuroscience and the Department of Molecular and Cellular Engineering, which is really the complement to our Gene Therapy Program. We did all of this in the last five years.

This overall integration of the new departments and the new centers and institutes with the old ones represents a major change in the infrastructure of the academic school.

In order to strengthen the support for our biomedical graduate students, we have tried to focus attention on three major areas. First, we have the joined under one superb person, Dr. Glenn Galton, the graduate program in biomedical research and the M.D./Ph.D. combined degree program. This reorganization was designed to eliminate the wasted energy and resources expended by two separate, competing programs. Second, we have expanded substantially our investment in graduate student support. Third, we have provided guaranteed support for junior faculty to take graduate students. Provided that a grant request has been submitted specifying graduate student support, we offer to pay for the graduate students until the grant is effected. This gives the new faculty some incentive and allows them to begin to take graduate students in their faculty careers.

The M.D./Ph.D. program is one of our most important programs. With about 11 or 12 students a year, it was probably either the first- or second -argest Medical Sciences Training Program (MSTP) in the country. However, because we have to turn away such fantastic applicants for this program, we resolved to find the funding to support additional students. In a major move, we have shifted up and expanded our commitment to support 30 M.D./Ph.D. students for as long as we can while we develop the training programs to underwrite the costs. This initiative will bring this program to encompass some 20% of the class. In fact, with 39 students entering this first year class and will have to back off from that. Even with 30 out of 150 students, it will probably be as large as any M.D./Ph.D. program in the country. This is a very successful program, and we are immensely pleased with it.

At the postdoctoral level, we have created an International Biomedical Scholars Program. Basically, we designed this to bring to Penn School of Medicine some outstanding people who will then return to develop faculty positions in one of the other major institutions of the world. What this program does is to provide matching support from Penn to help those institutions as their best people work over here. This program is just really getting off the ground. We do not know how well it will work. I am pleased that we have recruited to run this program Dr. Jim Wyngaarden, who was Director of the NIH for many years and most recently has been the Foreign Secretary for the National Academy of Sciences. He will be in a good position to be able to get in the doors to some of these institutions at the most senior levels and to really help us sell this program.

Clinical Research

We have put a great deal of effort into renovating, reorganizing, and expanding our General Clinical Research Center (GCRC), which, of course, is basically funded through the NIH's GCRC mechanism.

In addition to this, we have put a lot of effort into clinical research infrastructure. One of our major initiatives is the development of the Human Applications Laboratory. This is one of only two in the country. It is an FDA-approved mechanism to take gene therapy protocols from animal studies right to human studies. Jim Wilson set up the other human applications laboratory in Michigan, and then we recruited him to Penn to set up ours. Both of these laboratories are national laboratories, supported by the NIH to serve the entire country. We are pleased to be one of those laboratories and believe that this is extremely important as gene therapy continues to develop.

We have established an Investigational Drug Service and a Clinical Trials Coordinator office and we have recently initiated a task force to develop an aggressive plan to expand patient-related clinical research. This is an area that we think has received too little attention and one that has tremendous potential. We will put a great deal of effort into it.

We have experienced fairly substantial growth in the number of protocols, which means the number of patients and active clinical research going on in the institution have increased. The activity in the gene therapy area has stimulated a lot of this growth.

Faculty Support

We have done a number of things to try to make Penn a great place to be a faculty member. We have established an office of sponsored program services to provide specific support for faculty as they try to expand their research funding. We make available financial support of up to $10,000 for faculty planning new program projects.

We have done a great deal to enhance communication and information services in support of research and spent a lot of time and effort developing multiple core facilities. Among these core facilities are the Protein Chemistry Core, the DNA Chemistry Core, the High Capacity DNA Sequencing Core, and the Vector Construction Core for doing vector construction for gene therapy. We put a tremendous amount of effort into the development and support of these cores, and we are trying to do it even better than we have been.

In respect to our facilities, we did an analysis of the other medical institutions in our peer group in 1990 and concluded that we were way behind in research space. We have persuaded the university leadership and the trustees to support a long-range plan involving construction of several new research buildings. The first of those, the Stella Chance Laboratories, providing 200,000 gross square feet, was occupied in July 1994. This has provided space critical for the recruitment of six departmental chairs in some very important programs, three institute and center directors, and provided some other support space. The next new buildings, Biomedical Research Buildings 2 and 3, are envisioned to be nearly 400,000 gross square feet. These will provide incremental space, mostly for the basic science departments, but also for the multidisciplinary programs and for the clinical departments. This will allow us to rearrange a number of the departments, to bring them together where they are spread out in a variety of places, and provide space for core facilities and additional animal facilities. We have been working on that building for some time and began construction in spring of 1996. We are very excited about this and consider this as extremely important to our continued improvement in faculty research.

Data from the NIH on funding for schools of medicine shows that Penn is fifth in overall resear ch funding. Johns Hopkins, University of California, San Francisco, Washington University, and Yale, ranks in front of us. The School of Medicine, overall, has risen from 10th in 1990. We also pay attention to the position of each of our departments, and, with four exceptions, each of our departments is in the top ten. One of these is the Department of Medicine, which, after some major changes, has risen from 23rd to 6th. In addition, we have new chairs for each of the departments not in the top ten, and I expect each of those will be well into the top 10 soon. We are providing the resources to try to make this happen.

Last year, Penn School of Medicine had the highest annual growth rate for NIH funding among the top 10 institutions, having increased 11.4 percent in FY 1994–95. Penn's cumulative growth rate, in terms of total sponsored program dollars, has been about 11.8 percent since fiscal year 1989. Compared to the others in the top ten, Johns Hopkins was close behind us at 10.3 percent. We regard at this as pretty good, but believe we are just really getting things moving.

We had a major research retreat in April 1995, to focus on how to take advantage of new research opportunities as we move into this next era. One outcome of this was the recognition that we need to strive for the next level in our program to bring together research faculty who have never thought about doing research together. Several months ago, we started a program to review and approve applications for developing research areas that are not obviously related, but where people who are really creative could begin to think about ways to stimulate multidisciplinary programs. One example of this is the use of DNA instead of electronics as the mechanism of computing.

We want to be sure we provide oversight for the core facilities to make certain that they maximize their value. We want to make sure we take advantage of our managed-care environment in our health services research. We want to make sure that we are getting our students to go into science, and we want to enhance the way we work with our postdoctoral fellows as exemplified by our initiative with the international fellows described above. Very importantly in these activities, we want to really focus on patient-oriented clinical research where we see a tremendous opportunity.

Health Services

Health services takes most of our time and most of the time of most people who work in academic health centers. This is clearly where the biggest challenges exist today.

Our basic step in conceptualizing health services is to understand the market and try to make sure that we continue to understand the market. A model of market evolution that seems to hold up reasonably well is based on the assumption that the health-care market is in an evolutionary process, moving in some areas of the country faster than others. This model has four stages:

Stage 1   *The Unstructured Stage:* characterized by independent hospitals, independent physicians, unsophisticated purchasers— sort of the good old days as those of us in medicine often see it.

Stage 2   *The Loose Framework:* HMO enrollment, balloons, excess inpatient capacity in the hospitals, hospitals and physicians under price pressure, loose physician or provider networks, weak hospital affiliations.

Stage 3   *The Consolidation Phase:* a few large HMOs, PPOs emerge, network consolidation occurs, capitation of group practices, hospital margins erode, specialist revenue declines, integrated systems form.

Stage 4   *Managed Competition:* employers form coalitions to purchase health services and integrated systems manage patient populations.

Philadelphia is currently right in the middle of the second stage of this evolution. Places like Minneapolis, some places on the West Coast, or even Worcester, Massachusetts are far ahead. Other locations are still pretty primitive, such as Morgantown, West Virginia or Charlottesville, Virginia. But, it will not help to move there because they are not going to be at this stage long.

Understanding this environment led us to conclude that we had to have an integrated delivery system, and the key element for success lay in having a strong primary care network, which we lacked. This means that we also had to develop, throughout the region, the ability to have access to home care and outpatient programs, to care for patients within the community, to deliver cost-effective, high quality care, and to support this through outcomes measurement and patient satisfaction. It means focusing on prevention, health promotion, and health status, sharing risks throughout the system, and developing sophisticated information systems.

We began our health services strategic planning in September of 1991. We brought in our managers, faculty, and other administrative staff through two major retreats, one in January 1992 and one in June 1992, involving multiple leadership groups. That initial series of planning events led us to the following outcomes:

- We identified seven clinical program areas of emphasis
- We developed a distribution strategy that involved much more ambulatory care
- We wanted to improve the service that we were already providing; in other words, the established principles of practice
- We had to become much more aggressive in managed care
- We had to look at our affiliations differently
- We had to develop an aggressive management intervention plan to reduce cost
- Most importantly, we had to develop a health system

It was necessary at this stage to meet with various different committees and parts of the organization to get their buy-in to make the needed changes to develop the health system. We began extensive discussions with medical center leadership extending from November of 1992 until June of 1993. A week or two after this series of meetings began, we enlarged the orbit of our discussions to the medical center's academic leadership and faculty, and then, several weeks later, we began our discussions with the health system trustees. At this stage, we also had innumerable and extensive discussions with the university leadership, involving the president and executive vice president and other figures in the university community. This was a very long, drawn out, difficult process, but in the final analysis there is no question that the process was a tremendous help to us.

To demonstrate the dissimilarity between the psychology of academics and managers, in the summer of 1993, two weeks after we had finished this, when all of this was coming together and we had gotten final sign off from the trustees on our plan, one of our chairs called me and he said, "What are you doing?", and I said, "Well, we're implementing the plan that you and I have spent hundreds of hours going over." And there was dead silence on the other end, and he said, "Implementing?"

All of you are well aware of how academics operate. One's whole life is to put into getting that paper finished and published. Once the paper is published, you do not care what anybody does with it. You have done your thing. It is this same attitude toward strategic planning. Once you get the planning process done and it is put to paper, it is done. You do not have to worry about it. Going beyond this is a difficult shift for most in academia. They often do not seem to foresee that implementation is essential.

We got formal approval of the plan and began implementing it in June 1993. The plan led us to the following outcome: The medical center as it had existed prior to June of 1993—the Hospital of the University of Pennsylvania and the School of Medicine with its academic programs and its clinical departments or clinical practices—was combined with a health care network to become the University of Pennsylvania Health System. This health care network consisted of a primary care physician network, multispecialty satellites, a number of off-site ambulatory care facilities, multiple hospitals, a management services organization, and a managed care organization.

As CEO of the health system, I report to the President of the University. Our goal is to preserve and enhance our academic excellence in order to ensure access at a reasonable cost to a sufficient number and diversity of patients for educational programs. All of the effort to decide what kind of network we needed was based on the institution's educational mission. In other words, we performed the market research to see what we should do to support what the clinical chairs had told us was needed, from an educational perspective, in order to have one of the top five academic training programs in each of their disciplines. We needed to create a network that met the requirements of managed competition for a regionally coordinated delivery system that provided the highest quality care and service in a full range of clinical services, was geographically distributed throughout the region, and was cost-effective. We had to have adequate control over the system elements to ensure that we met our academic and clinical standards, and we had to assure our financial viability.

Each component in the system faced a particular major issue: cost reduction. Cost reduction has been the major issue with the Hospital of the University of Pennsylvania. In 1989, the Hospital of the University of Pennsylvania was regarded as the most expensive hospital in the United States. Being at the top in this particular category is not an achievement in which we take great pride, so we very aggressively have pursued an expense reduction program while, at the same time, preserving and enhancing the quality of care and service. Since 1989, we have taken out $65 million of recurring expenditures, and the FY97 budget will increase this reduction to a total of $75 million. This is about 15 percent of the expense budget of the hospital. Using a cost per case index that relates costs based on the complexity of the patient cases, the Hospital of the University of Pennsylvania is now the least expensive university hospital in Philadelphia, although we are still more expensive than a number of the good community hospitals in the region. We have been successful in cost reduction and that has been immensely important to our continued ability to operate in the black. This process continues.

The biggest challenge in respect to clinical practices is somehow to turn them from fiercely competitive entities that are independent of each other, independent of the institution, and feel threatened by loss of their independence, into multispecialty group practices. We are now moving very rapidly in this, and part of our plan is an expense reduction of $30 million per annum by FY99. That is about 15 percent of the expense budget. While this is initial, it no doubt will be the most difficult thing we have to do.

As part of our strategy, our subspecialists are developing networks involving the subspecialties in the region that complement our health system. Indeed, there are a number of the different network strategies that are ongoing in the clinical departments. Two examples are:

The Cancer Network. The cancer program has developed a linkage with about twenty-three different community hospitals in the region, where we participate in the care of tertiary and quaternary patients. We have built up a good collaborative clinical and research linkage, and the affiliated physicians and hospitals cooperate with us in a number of protocols.

This program, which brings together a number of hospitals and oncologists throughout eastern Pennsylvania and parts of New Jersey, has been extremely important to us.

Telaquest. Represents another approach. This new company is a national telaradiology consortium established and owned by the radiology departments of six institutions, including Penn, that offers subspecialty consultation to providers of high-tech imaging services. For example, when one wants to read a CT or MRI or PET scan, the participating institutions can provide many experts dedicated to interpreting the specific images. One can very easily transmit these scans electronically to the member institutions. This also provides educational material for the residents and the students. Telaquest, although designed to sustain and enhance our educational research programs, is organized as a for-profit organization and represents a model for national consortia that may be applicable to other clinical disciplines.

The component of the new University of Pennsylvania Health System that represents the biggest challenge was the Primary Care Physician Network. By far, this is our most important strategic initiative. In order to maintain a flow of patients throughout the whole system, we need a geographically distributed group of primary care physicians to provide health care services. Solution of this missing link will allow us to accept risk-capitated contracts with HMOs. These contracts pay a percentage of the premiums to the provider organizations. The PCP Network will also allow us to enrich our student and resident education programs by providing mentors and role models for students considering careers in primary care. We sized the Primary Care Physician Network on this basis. The greater Philadelphia area has about 6 million people. We sized-out our program to cover about 800,000 lives, or about 15 percent of this population. This would require about 400 primary care physicians. When we started with five, we had a long way to go.

First, we took the five southeastern Pennsylvania counties, three counties in southern New Jersey, and one county in northern Delaware and began to identify the areas where we needed primary care physicians. We attempted to identify the best primary care physicians in those areas and began to acquire their practices. Philadelphia County has been nicely populated, and we have quite good coverage now in Montgomery, Chester, and Bucks counties, in Pennsylvania. We have begun good penetration in Mercer County, New Jersey, but less so in some of the other counties. We're at about 200 physicians who have now joined us in the health system and believe that it has moved well.

We knew we were going to need off-site ambulatory care facilities in addition to this network of physicians. We have now acquired about seventy-five primary care sites and expect to have about seventy eventually. We also needed to develop three or four multispecialty satellites distributed around the region to handle the patients who did not wish to come for care into central Philadelphia. The first of those satellites is in Radnor, Pennsylvania, close to a major new highway there. It occupies a 170,000 square foot building and, when it is fully mature, will accommodate about thirty-eight physician FTEs and some 300,000 patient visits a year. Bucks County and Burlington County, New Jersey will be future sites.

Prior to 1994, our patient volume was steady, in the 500,000 to 550,000 visit range. This does not include pediatrics, which is served through Children's Hospital and reported separately. As we have begun to build our network, we have seen these numbers go up sharply. We are projecting this year about 1.6 million visits. In addition, admissions at Hospital of the University of Pennsylvania also are the largest in the history of the hospital. So we have done a good job of expanding our volume of patients at a time when most institutions are having a great deal of difficulty in doing this.

The second primary care strategy we developed was the Management Services Organization. This is a for-profit entity set up to serve independent physicians—those who have decided against joining a system. What we discovered in our market research was that these unaffiliated physicians have a tremendous problem since they could not contract effectively with managed care organizations. In addition to improving this, we could help with patient scheduling, registration, office management, purchasing, facilities management, and so on. This, in turn, would allow the physicians to spend their time taking care of patients instead of having to deal with the ever increasing hassles of the current health-care business environment. The Management Services Organization will also have a real marketing synergy with Clinical Care Associates, which is our primary care organization. The sales activities have just begun this fall, and we expect it to be fully operational by next summer. We expect that the whole system will be fully developed by the year 2000.

We have acquired a new hospital, but this is simply because it is right on the campus, and we thought it was important to prevent someone else from acquiring it. As a rule, however, owning other hospitals is not critical to us. Our strategy is to try to select four to six of the best community hospitals in order to provide high quality teaching sites for us that are complementary to the university hospital. We then look to partner with them and work with them as part of our team. This is a vertical integration strategy. It offers our patients the most appropriate, most convenient, most cost-effective settings for care. It creates linkages with our Primary Care Physician Network and allows us to achieve geographic distribution of our clinical service requirements. It will permit other kinds of vertical integration, such as with nursing homes, long-term care and home care organizations. If, at some point, a merger of assets becomes attractive to both parties, then our experience as partners will be helpful in guiding any future discussions.

We have decided not to get into the intense and rapidly growing managed-care business ourselves. Instead, we are attempting to work out long-term joint ventures with as many of the major insurers as possible. Because the physicians work directly with us, we can manage our patients as well as or better than a managed-care organization. We now have a large, organized, provider system and a substantial managed-care infrastructure including people who can negotiate contracts with managed-care organizations on a basis of strength. We have contracts with a number of HMOs that are "full risk" in nature.

Here are two examples of how this health system can help our research and educational programs.

With our system in place, we can begin to look at issues such as how to implement the tremendous advances in human genetics and apply this to a patient population. Last year alone some fourteen new diseases were defined at the level of the gene. This year the numbers will be higher, and this number will continue to explode. The advances in genetics, and the ability to do things as a result of this new understanding, will far exceed any physician or genetic counselor's ability to manage the new information. So what can we do in this? First of all, we can take a look at enhancing our DNA diagnostic capabilities and organizing our system so that we can provide genetic counseling and education in this new era. For example, what do you do with the breast cancer 1 gene? Who needs this test? What do you do with the information if the results are positive? Who needs genes tested for colon cancer? We believe that because of the network we have developed and our tremendous academic strengths, we are able to focus in this area in a way that far exceeds what any group of physicians or hospitals alone are going to be able to achieve.

Health-services research is another special strength of our system. Through the Leonard Davis Institute and other parts of our organization, we have more than 100 faculty that concentrate on outcomes research. This work can be directed to our patient population. This, in effect, becomes their laboratory. There are other areas, as well, such as diseases management and translational medicine that require an integrated academic health system to be marginally successful.

We think that we can develop a model that demonstrates the unique value of an academic integrated health-care delivery system that will guide public policy in the development of a national health-care delivery system. We think we can develop and implement a medical education curriculum that will also serve as a national example, as well. All these outcomes are critical to us because they support our basic mission, which is the preservation and continued enhancement of our academic excellence.

DISCUSSION

You have shown pretty convincingly that the first requirement for improving academic excellence is the recruitment of the best scientists. Recruitment, as we all find out, requires a tremendous amount of capital, especially at the top of fields that are very competitive. At our institution, the capital to provide this margin is driven by the wealth that we can generate in the political enterprise. Furthermore, as we compete in a national market for faculty, we are competing in regional markets for health care. Different people operate in different territories. So, in part, people have different wealth. Finally, the health system itself requires a vast reinvestment of wealth; buying all those primary-care practices might be an example of this. So, based on these facts, I have two questions.

First, how do you balance reinvestment of money in the health-care business versus investment in research?

Secondly, in the research mission, is there a way to husband resources by focusing more selectively? You noted that you chose eight areas of research focus. What did you not choose? Are there fields you just have to cover?

Kelley: I think one of the things that is most important in the organization is that the trustees and the university leadership decided in the mid-1980s that the medical center ought to be under one physician leader. Although this decision has been questioned periodically, we continue to conclude that we need to keep the organization unified. In my view, this is extremely important.

Right now the only part of an organization that has any kind of positive financial margin to speak of is the hospital. As long as we are able to reduce costs aggressively and continue to improve quality, this situation should last for a while. We are taking advantage of this by investing some the capital in health services and the research and education programs. Were we not a unified organization, we would not have access to this hospital resource.

My heart and soul are in the academic mission. I worry about every nickel that I have to spend that is not spent in academia. So, when we expend resources to build our network, it's only after we have decided that there is no other way. Many, I know, view spending in education as a necessary expense of doing business rather than as an investment in the future. These individuals have difficulty truly supporting the academic mission.

So, by keeping our resources together and allocating them as we believe that we must, we have been able to preserve a fair amount to support the research mission. This does not mean just the research mission in the medical school. We believe we have supported the research mission throughout the university, and this is good for everybody.

Your presentation highlighted very clearly the consolidation that is occurring in the whole health services sector. We see it among HMOs, we see it among hospitals, we are seeing it very rapidly now among physicians. We've, of course, seen it among pharmaceutical companies, hospital supply companies, and medical device companies. The whole industry is consolidating as each sector seeks to maintain its competitive edge in respect to customers, vendors, and so forth. This forces a university that is in the academic medical area to make a decision about whether it's going to be a consolidator or consolidatee, an acquirer or an acquiree. They have to make this decision. Nearly every university in the country that now owns and operates a teaching hospital is going through a soul-searching exercise to determine which way they are going to go.

Now, capital somewhat limits this choice. In the case of Penn, you clearly have a very profitable hospital that has been able to generate a sizable amount of free cash that you can reinvest into the development of your broad system. Most teaching hospitals simply are not that profitable. Therefore, most universities, although they would prefer to be a consolidator, they simply do not have the capital to do this. So, we see numerous universities either look at entry into joint ventures with stronger strategic partners that have access to capital, or, in some cases, actually sell their hospital to one of the hospital management companies.

I think it might be helpful if you just comment on this dilemma that universities face, and tell what advice you would give those universities that do not have the access to capital.

Kelley: Glenn Stein and I were at Penn in 1989 when the hospital had just lost $14 million in operations, and the trustees were absolutely beside themselves because things were totally out of control in the hospital. Not only had we lost

$14 million in 1988, but $6 million were lost in the month of June that nobody had predicted and nobody could understand.

Glenn was the Budget Director at Penn at this extremely difficult time. The benefit for me was that I came into the situation after these losses had occurred. Therefore, I was enabled to make a lot of changes that would not have been acceptable had this not been a crisis situation.

The trustees had not believed they were ever going to run into such a deficit, nor did they believe that any management could ever correct it. There was tremendous concern about this. However, simple good management has made us very successful. We brought in superb people who knew how to manage the hospital, and we are doing a million things differently. That has made a tremendous difference, and many of the academic institutions in this country could do as well. Certainly, every environment is a bit different, but ours is not any easier than most of them.

I know that a number of institutions are looking at ways to sell their hospitals, and I think that this a big mistake. Certainly others have different views. However, I think that any institution that spins off their hospital or their practices is going to end up having to buy back those services from those same hospitals and those physicians sooner or later, and maybe a lot sooner. The days of separate hospitals and physicians being willing to give their time and money to support the academic mission are coming to an end. If they are not part of you, they are not going to be willing to give you their resources. Certainly, the HMOs are not willing to put anything substantial into education and research. To the extent that HMOs control, as they will be doing increasingly, the bottom lines of physicians and hospitals, medical schools without hospitals will face serious problems.

So your recommendation would be to focus on management of the hospital, make it more profitable, and use those earnings to support the academic mission?

Let me follow up with a brief comment on that. I spent nine years as a hospital administrator. So I used to be one of those people who thought every penny should be reinvested in hospital operations. Now, as a university CFO, I agree with Dr. Kelley that every penny can come back into education and research.

Kelley: Two really important points that I have certainly learned during the last couple of years are:

> First, despite all the pressures, hospitals and health care can be well managed and, when you are ahead of the curve, can be very profitable enterprises. A hospital should be viewed as an asset, not as a liability or a

potential liability to universities and to the academic mission. I would encourage university leadership to try to retain the hospital and the health-care institution within their enterprise and not sell it off, give it away, or whatever someone else may be doing.

Secondly, it is very important for the CEO of the academic medical center to play the strong shareholder role, whether that shareholder is a for-profit company or a university, as in the case of Penn. Otherwise, there will be a tremendous temptation to fight the last war, which often means to over-reinvest in the the wrong thing. So, playing that role, being able to take the margins you can make and using them to support the academic mission in a very rigorous way, I think, is very important. This is certainly the course that Penn has followed.

Two questions:
First, why do you acquire primary care practices rather than simply capitate positions?
Secondly, I really do not understand how you have been able to almost triple outpatient visits during this time period, when you are now managing only about 29,000 lives on a capitated basis. In a community that obviously has a lot of managed care volume, are you doing it with pricing other HMOs, or what?

Kelley: The reason we decided to go the acquisition route was that when we looked around the country at what others had done in trying to link with primary care physicians, we found that links short of the acquisition process with primary care physicians did not stick.

We discovered, for example, one institution that spent a great deal of time contracting with seventy or eighty primary-care physicians. An HMO came into town and, literally, within a week, had totally destroyed this whole network of relationships by offering these physicians significant payments, equity participation, and other inducements. All the effort that had gone into building this network structure was destroyed overnight.

Our acquisition agreement entails both a long-term commitment and a non-compete clause that stipulates that when and if we terminate the agreement, the physician, for a period of years, cannot practice within a specified number of miles from the particular practice site. We thought that this was an important element to maintain a strong structure with sufficient commitment to make the arrangement work. One thing we have learned in developing the system is that the participants do not necessarily feel an urge to cooperate. So, if one does not have the greater degree of control so as to be able to force an issue, you will never get the system to work.

I am certain now that the decision to undertake the acquisition process was very important to us. I believe, too, that a strategy to start up new practices will actually cost you more than the acquisition of physicians' practices that are already there.

As to patient volume, we probably have a million patients that we are taking care of that represent those 1.4 million visits. However, we have a very small percentage at this stage that is really capitated, about 29,000. Part of the reason is that we have just started. I am sure this figure will become greater. Actually, we do not want it to get too high, because if this becomes the dominant form of payment, it will be very difficult for us.

Your comment was that if your number of capitated patients increases, you will be in trouble. I am linking this with your comments about how maturation of the health-care system would head towards capitation and your decision not to compete with HMOs. Can you clarify the relationships in all this?

Kelley: Right now capitated lives are all incremental to us. Every 100,000 lives are worth $100 million a year in incremental revenues. Because we have a big fixed cost base, that this capitated portion stays incremental is important. As we take care of more and more patients in the hospital, the incremental expense for this is probably only 20 percent of the revenue because of the fixed cost. If we were to get into a situation where we were 80 or 90 percent capitated, then we would have significant issues in terms of how to manage that with our current cost base unless we could get it down significantly. At that level, we would be displacing patients with other coverage, and it would not be incremental. So, we really must continue to have other kinds of patients to be able to stay in the black.

On the other hand, if we had not had the ability to take risk contracts, we would have been out of business a decade earlier. Risk contracts exist when you take risk for a patient, the responsibility for the health care of that patient, at a percentage of premium with the HMO. A large primary-care network and the ability to provide a full range of services, such as long-term care, home care, and other kinds of services are required in order to do this successfully. If an organization does not have this system in place and, so, can not take risk contracts, all it can do is deal on specialty contracts or the per diems, both of which can be financially devastating. Risk contracts have been the most attractive arrangements recently. Health-care managers on the West Coast with whom we have spoken have said, "If you can do risk contracts, this is by far the way to go." We believe that very few health systems will actually be able to handle full risk contracts with single signature authority.

Why we do not get into the HMO business ourselves is very clear. The two dominant HMOs in Philadelphia would have put us out of business instantaneously. If we were in a less mature market this decision might be different. An organization such as ours certainly cannot do this in Philadelphia. However, we are building the infrastructure of managed care. So, if someday the HMOs are not willing to deal with us in an appropriate way, we conceivably could move ahead, be our own HMO, and directly contract with employers. Nevertheless, we do not particularly want to do this. We do not think that the marketing, claims processing, and so on, are activities in which we want to be experts. However, the fact that they know that we could work as an HMO is good leverage.

What sort of agreement do you have with the managed-care providers that they are willing to allow you to migrate, if you will, to fixed cost, rather than go after you and say, "You are a high cost provider, and we are going to take advantage of it?"

Kelley: I think the HMOs are ambivalent about these risk contracts. I understand that in some areas they are unwilling to do these agreements. On the other hand, because it takes all their risk away, and really assures a predictable profitability for them that they otherwise lack, they usually are eager to take the opportunity.

Do you find you are able to find high quality physicians from the areas you need?

Kelley: Absolutely.

You did not buy hospitals?

Kelley: No, except for one hospital that was on campus that we were anxious not to be sold to somebody else. We are not trying to buy hospitals. We think in the long run that we must have community hospitals with whom we work well. If we need to own them to do this, then we probably will.

In the volume increase at the Hospital of the University of Pennsylvania, have you had a significant shift in case specs? Are you seeing more acute patients coming into HUP?

Kelley: Yes, our case-mix indexes continue to go up every year.

So, you are really becoming a teaching institution?

Kelley: Yes, more and more tertiary all the time.

Do you have a pie chart to show where the resources come from to support this incredible enterprise on an operating basis each year?

Kelley: This would be extremely easy to execute. 100 percent of our flexible resources come from the hospital. That is an easy pie chart without a little sliver in there of anything else. It is entirely the hospital operations that have allowed us to do this.

You have no debt at all?

Kelley: Well, we have. We did issue some bonds last year, but our cash reserves are far greater than our debt. We are borrowing money, but we have lots of cash with which to work.

With the margins that U.S. Healthcare and some of these other HMOs are getting off the top, though, this is not going to last for very long.

Kelley: You mean the 31 percent? We are not going to take a contract where we get 69 percent of the premium either.

Do you think it's inevitable that you are going to have to move up the feeding chain?

Kelley: We are committed to staying out of the HMO business. If someday we are forced to reconsider, we will decide on it then. However, we are not wasting a lot of time on it.

What is the way you are dealing with the major government cutbacks in federal funding for graduate medical education?

Kelley: The bills that are passing in Congress right now cause us deep concern. Some of the proposed hits look as if they could take away from us as much as $80 million a year. Right now, it looks closer to $25 million a year, but, still, that is a lot of money. I do not know exactly how this is going to work out with all of the threats that are circulating. However, I think virtually every academic health center in the country can be in the red if they are not careful. All of us have benefited from the indirect medical education payments, the direct medical education payments and the disproportionate share. If we lose as much as the proposed bills are looking to cut, it is going to be a tremendous hit.

Pretend I am a junior congressman from Montana, and I want to flip to the research side, which relates to what you just said. Now, Penn is trying hard

and successfully in becoming a better research facility, going from 15th to 8th in the past decade. You do this by attracting and recruiting, at higher salaries faculty from other very fine institutions. Again, as a junior congressman, I see that the top five highly compensated people at Pennsylvania and the other research institutions are all doctors. What do you say to that congressman when he suggests that all you are doing is just upping the ante and putting it on the U.S. taxpayer?

Kelley: The position that we emphasize is that we have been enabled to start programs, such as our Gene Therapy Program, in which the first ever successful gene therapy was conducted, and where we have fifteen different clinical protocols now in development. Two clinical studies will begin in the next several weeks. One, in mesothelioma, and the other, in brain tumors. There are going to be cures and prevention that will come out of our Gene Therapy Program that is going to help the health of everyone in the world, including everybody in Montana. This is worth the investment that they are making, particularly given that it is a very small investment, and the return is literally orders and orders of magnitude greater than the investment.

An institution like Penn is uniquely motivated and organized to foster the initiation of programs that are born out of pure research. Once these programs are begun, we are able to keep them funded, but nobody is willing to pay to get them started. Initiatives of this kind have to come out of educational and research institutions. If this entire institutional research base is destroyed, which could happen in a year or two or three, we will lose our ability to be the leader in the world in biomedical research. We then will be unable to support the improvement of health care or to help in the translation of research through to the pharmaceutical industry or the biotechnology industry where we also are still the world leaders. Thus, our global leadership position in biomedical research, health care, and the commercial sector of human health will be destroyed. We will be repeating our mistakes in the electronics industry or the computer industry. We face a tremendous threat to an enterprise in which we have been the undisputed world leader, and this is a jeopardy to our nation. That is what I would tell the junior congressman from Montana.

The model of a strong CEO of a unified academic medical center at Chicago is called the Kelley Model. A lot of people spend a great amount of time asking if the reason that the Kelley Model works is because of Kelley or because of the model. What can other universities learn about planning and the management and leadership of complex institutions from academic medical centers? Do you have any insight into that for us?

Kelley: There are many great people in American medicine who do the same thing that I do. Many of them are placed in tremendously difficult, if not impossible, situations of because the dean and the CEO of the hospital are out to destroy each other. It is virtually impossible for any two people to work together in this situation where the incentives may be so different, the interfaces so vast, and the conflicts so frequent. The best people in the country placed in that role will not succeed. If you are spending all your time worrying about how to protect yourself from that other guy, and he is spending all his time worried about how to protect himself or take advantage of you, you can not develop a vision, implement it, and make things happen. This divided type of organization is not going to work in the next era.

Is there an alternative that could be constructed to the proposition that you want to educate 400 University of Pennsylvania students in medicine, but to do this, you must play into this brilliant strategy to provide health care to one out of every five people in the metropolitan area, a mission larger than the rest of the university probably had the capital to take over? An option is to not educate those 400 students.

Kelley: That is an option.

Another option, if you wish to retain your medical school, is to just have your medical school and get rid of all the rest of the apparatus. I call this the Harvard Model. However, I do not believe that the Harvard Model is going to work very much longer. The involved hospitals are going to start saying to the medical school, "Hey, guys, you know we're tired of donating our time and effort to you. It costs us 35 percent more to run this hospital because of all those students," and the involved physicians will say, "Hey, we do not have any time. The HMO is telling us exactly how many minutes we can spend with each patient. We could not possibly use this time to teach unless you are willing to pay for it. And, oh, by the way, you are collecting $25,000 a year from each of those students. Where's our share? We're doing all the teaching." It's just inevitable that this is going to happen, as far as I can see.

I think that the prestige factor of a medical school linkage has been very important in attracting patients. However, this will fade as the patients are directed to choose medical care on the basis of the physician or hospital being part of an HMO. When you are part of this contract, and it does not make much difference whether you have Harvard medical students or not, the incentive to spend time or resources to preserve the association will disappear. I think we are going to start seeing a real change in attitude there. So, if it is not your organization, you are going to have to pay for it. Then, the crucial decision is going to be whether the university can afford to have a medical school. I bet some places that get into that situation are going to decide that they cannot.

If you are in a position five years from now in which you are taking capitation on 600,000 lives, you are, in essence, functioning as a wholesale

HMO. **So, you are taking risk, substantial risk. From the perspective of the university, your operations now may account for maybe 80 or 85 percent of the university's operations as a whole, in terms of revenues, investments, and so forth. So if anything goes wrong, for example, you take the wrong capitation rate or your actuarial analysis is incorrect, this has major ramifications for the entire university. I wonder to what extent your own trustees have thought about and addressed this issue?**

Kelley: A lot. We have had a lot of discussion about this, and I think this is a very important concern. It really is a matter of what are the risks versus the benefits of doing it this way versus that way. There certainly are risks. This is going to be a question that every university with a medical school is going to need to deal with.

You talked about financial incentives for the new clinical chairs you appointed. How about financial incentives for administrators in your Health Services Organization? Do you have incentive compensation? Then, how would you deal with the issue if the dean of arts and sciences says, "Well if they do it over at the medical school, I want to pay my budget director a bonus for keeping our costs under control," and on, and on, and on.

Kelley: We have provided an incentive program for approximately forty of the top senior people in the administration of the health system. Eleven of those administrators are direct reports to me, and the rest report to people under me. About half of the incentive is a group incentive based on a set of group criteria that we have agreed makes sense. The rest is an individual incentive based on each individual program.

In addition to this, we have done the same with the clinical chairs. They are eligible for 50 percent as a group incentive to achieve some things we are trying to achieve, for example, the consolidation of the group practice approach.

Group practice consolidation is extremely important to us. It is going to happen as fast as we can make it happen, and we are putting substantial personal incentives in for the clinical chairs to be a part of it.

I think it works. To be honest with you, I have been really amazed at how well it works. We have had some of our greatest success with chairs where we have developed the incentive to improve what they were not doing well. For example, if service in a department was awful, we tied a big piece of the incentive to improvement of service. If during the first year, service was still awful, the chair got barely any incentive that year. He or she must have been very upset. I guarantee that this chair, from this point on, is paying a whole lot more attention to service than before. It has worked well even with people who are doing an excellent job. The trick is to find where they are not doing an excellent job and put the main incentives there, but put a little bit elsewhere to help them maintain their excellence in other areas.

While this is unusual in academic institutions, I think it is going to happen in more institutions, probably very swiftly. Certainly for us it has been extremely important.

Do you think that in the area of research, competition between your institution and the pharmaceutical industry and various biomedical industries may be developing, that you may be in a position where you are each doing what the other is doing, and that there will be a battle that will focus on increases to research tax credits versus NIH funding and federal research grants?

Kelley: Part of the clinical research task force that we have put together is to address this very issue of the black hole that exists between academic research and industry.

I had the good fortune of serving on a couple of corporate boards, including Merck & Company, so I know a little bit about their research enterprise and how they do things. Any of the major pharmaceutical companies is going to invest in drugs that have a large potential market.

The biotechnology companies, on the other hand, will take on a small product, but for them their whole survival is usually dependent on the success of that one product. So this gives them a particular view of how important the success of that product is.

From the academic perspective, we generally will take our research only so far, publish the results, and then we may or may not decide to pursue this research any more. We may be done with it.

There is, in this system, a black hole consisting of all of the tremendously exciting things that could be, but are never going to be, developed because academia will not take the research far enough, and industry does not perceive any reason to pick it up. I think that academia ought to begin to approach this black hole, not as a competitor to industry, but to fill the role of bringing research a little bit further along. There is a tremendous amount that academia can do to take research a little bit farther so that it will be easier for the commercial sector to see potential value and complete the competitive product development process.

I mentioned our Gene Therapy Program and our Human Applications Laboratory. These are good examples of what can be done. The Human Applications Laboratory is FDA-approved. So we can take vectors into that lab, develop them for human use, and begin human studies with those vectors. For example, we began clinical studies in cystic fibrosis with our own vector developed at Penn by our Institute of Human Gene Therapy people. No industry had invested in this vector. As we began our first clinical studies, it was clear that this vector was going to be a problem. It was not going anywhere. We stopped the studies, redesigned the vector, and went back to animal, primate, and human studies with the next generation vector.

The way it usually works in America right now is that a company has a vector and gives that vector to the investigators at University X to do the clinical studies. If this company has its whole future based on the success of this vector, it may not stop the studies, go back, and redesign the vector, or, if it does, it is going to be a very difficult decision.

This is a way that clinical research can evolve from academia to cover that black hole, not to compete with industry, but to take things further along the path so that industry will see that the principle has been proven. We are able to take this research forward because of the service itself, without concern about the potential size of the market.

I see this as an area where we are certainly going to be doing more. I expect this to be an outcome of our clinical research task force, and I do not see this as at all competitive with industry. Rather, I see this as very complementary and helpful in getting more research findings out of the academic institutions into improving human health.

Would you continue to capitalize these activities through government funding or would you look for private investments?

Kelley: The start-up is what is expensive. Once the research starts, then it will likely will be supported by the NIH, another nonprofit grant source, or possibly some industry sources. It is much easier to support research once it's started and shows promise.

Chapter 4

::

From Shared Governance to Shared Responsibility:

The Great and Painful Labor of Adaptation Has Begun

Stephen Joel Trachtenberg, **The George Washington University**

::

AMERICANS "LOSE PATIENCE" WITH THEIR SCHOOLS OF HIGHER EDUCATION

"Towers of Babble" was the title of the article. It appeared in the issue of *The Economist* dated December 15, 1993–January 7, 1994. And like all *Economist* articles, it strove for the heft of a definitive summing-up: The "last word" on a subject already familiar to its weighty international audience.

"Universities are on the defensive everywhere," the text declared, "distrusted by governments, worried about losing income and influence. In Germany, politicians complain that revitalizing the East will be a doodle compared with reforming the campus. In the United States, the post of university president has been reduced from one of the most pleasant to one of the most irksome positions around. In Britain, the government treats higher education like an inefficient nationalized industry."

Worst of all, the article said, officials on both sides of the Atlantic, in their rising tide of displeasure, are only expressing, and acting upon, the outraged feelings of their constituents: "Nothing less than a populist backlash against academia appears to be under way. Politicians win easy applause by ridiculing the silliest bits of academic research. Pundits lampoon this or that bit of PC (politically correct) intolerance. Publishers churn out books with titles like *Tenured Radicals* and *Impostors in the Temple*. And in addition to the complaint that universities "have been hijacked by 1960's radicals, more intent on pandering to minorities than advancing knowledge," the voters of the Western nations are increasingly convinced that academics rarely give value for money. Parents and students often make huge sacrifices for a university education. In return they get indifferent teaching and crowded libraries. These problems are particularly serious in America, where fees are exorbitant, star professors are perpetually on sabbatical, and much of the teaching is done by graduate students (many with a poor command of English).

At a time when think-tanks, the media, and new information technologies are making academia "less central to intellectual life," *The Economist* reported, schools of higher education are increasingly "confused about their mission and even their legitimacy." In the United States—once the global inspiration where higher education was concerned—"federal and state governments cut spending on higher education and parents balk at soaring fees . . . Governments, which foot much of the (academic) bill, are increasingly keen to know how their money is spent."

The results, according to *The Economist*, are apparent:

> Everywhere, universities are introducing tighter management, treating dons like employees rather than gentleman-scholars, paying star performers star salaries and, even more controversially, contracting out more of their teaching and research to non-tenured staff. . . . Today, universities must adapt to a world in which governments are reluctant to fund higher education: in which students are as likely to be middle-aged managers, trying to update their skills or change their careers, as impressionable school-leavers; and in which knowledge-intensive industries, happily innocent of lifetime tenure and union-negotiated pay-scales, are competing to buy talent.

I have quoted the 1993–94 issue of *The Economist* at such length because it sets an important floor under future debates about what faculty members and administrators must do in order to preserve their paychecks and at least a portion—a carefully selected portion—of their present professional environment. They must,to use *The Economist*'s key word, *adapt.* Specifically, they must adapt to their sponsoring societies, whose individual citizens now confront a world economy in which the drive for self-preservation is mandated by the Darwinian grimness of the wages of personal and/or national failure.

They must do, in short, what they have so often done before.

AMERICAN COLLEGES AND UNIVERSITIES AS ENGINES OF ADAPTATION

Those of us who attended a liberal arts college within a much larger university in the 1950's can remember a moment in academic history when authority, morale, and power were almost visibly draining from the former into the latter. At Columbia, where I experienced my own higher education between 1955 and 1959, the allegorical figure caught at the transitional divide was a young professor of the liberal arts generally acknowledged to be one of the college's very best instructors. And not only that. He was also a figure in the school's "great tradition," having attended Columbia as an undergraduate, having gained as a mentor one of its most talented senior professors, and having received—as the latter did, twenty years earlier—one of its prized postgraduate scholarships for study at a major British university.

But young Professor X had a problem: a writing-block so severe that he simply could not finish a dissertation and a Ph.D. In the prewar and immediate postwar period that might not have proven an insuperable problem. In the later 1950s, it was definitely becoming one. The years dragged by. The authorities at the college, and at its parent university, agonized and temporized. And at last, young Professor X was denied tenure and had to leave, notwithstanding the belated completion of his doctorate.

"I happened to spot him in the hallway of 'the department' on a spring day just after classes had ended," a Columbia friend recently wrote me. "There wasn't a soul around. I myself was there, probably, to shove some communication or other under somebody's door. And there he was, just drifting slowly down the hallway, motes of dust dancing in the sunshine from the windows, and the old oak-framing of the office doors actually glowing a bit under their archaic coatings of varnish. If he saw me—and I do vaguely remember saying hello to him—he didn't really register my presence. He was saying good-bye. He was an astronaut embarked for some colder planet, and he was bidding a plangent farewell to his home."

From the perspective of 1994, Professor X, who died prematurely of lung cancer after enjoying a splendid career revival at an independent liberal arts college, could easily be seen as part of an American tragicomedy. "Great teaching" was fading out as an American ideal—an ideal so strong that even *Esquire* magazine once ran a major article on the nation's "greatest college teachers"—and was being replaced by a pervasive hunger for the Nobel Prize, or the closest approximation thereof, and for everything that fell under the heading of "research." In this new world, the Ph.D. was an indispensable ticket of admission. And in this new world, many of those teaching at the staunchest liberal arts colleges would slowly begin to remodel themselves along university lines. In the liberal arts college as in the massive university, status began to accrue to the faculty members with the most impressive extramural (i.e., national and international) reputations. Status slowly but surely departed from the faculty members who *only* devoted themselves to their teaching and their students, as well as "service to the institution."

But from the perspective of 1994, this process, so visible and apparently relentless in the late 1950s and early 1960s, can be seen in retrospect as an inevitable adaptation to *the wishes of the American people*. The Second World War had been won, after all, through the exercise of the graduate-school virtues. Scientific research had produced the atomic bomb. Highly advanced training in Japanese and German, conducted at an unprecedented pace, had enabled Americans to meet and to match their European and Asian adversaries. Machines rather than poems, steel crafted in factories rather than paintings hung in museums, had enabled this nation to fight and win a "two-front" war of unprecedented savagery. And the subsequent Cold War was commonly perceived as a scientific and technological struggle in which even stalemate could only be purchased through an immense investment in advanced knowledge.

From the American people, therefore, our schools of higher education received a clear, sharp signal. Americans were willing to support everything represented by "Harvard." They wanted their own children to "go to Harvard"—or as near as possible—even after it was made quite clear to them that regular, intimate seminars with John Kenneth Galbraith were not likely to figure among their children's everyday Harvard experiences. As the 1950s drew to a close, therefore, and the 1960s began, only minutes seemed to pass before a "research model" was taking over even in university departments teaching liberal arts subjects to undergraduates and, to a steadily growing extent, even in independent liberal arts colleges. American schools of higher education adapted, in a way that made perfect sense, to the ideological signals they were receiving—together with very large amounts of money—from their benefactors. With the passage by Congress of the National Defense Education Act (NDEA), even the teaching of foreign languages became a matter of "national defense," just like nuclear physics.

And the results of this act of adaptation have been genuinely impressive. In their collective sense that the world had entered an age of science and technology, and that American schools of higher education needed to acknowledge that fact, Americans were quite correct. Clark Kerr points out in his most recent book that in the twentieth century, "in some twenty-five hundred leading journals in fields of science, one-third of all articles have been written by Americans and one-half of all citations are to contributions made by Americans, although the United States has only 5 percent of the world population."[1] Of the Nobel Prizes awarded through 1990 in physics, chemistry, physiology/medicine, and economics, Americans won fifty-three. The runners-up are West Germany (ten), the United Kingdom (seven), and Sweden (four).

Facts like these are reasonably well-known. What needs to be acknowledged is that the establishment of this record would have been inconceivable without the active participation of American universities as sponsors of research, and that this role, in turn, required the active and tacit approval of the American people.

The research-generating subsidies provided between 1950 and the early 1980s to the University of California, the University of Texas, the State University of New York, the University of Michigan, and other major institutions struck the citizens of those states, and most Americans paying their federal taxes, as money essentially well-invested. To an extent that seems quite enviable from our present perspective, schools of higher education adapted to the perceived desires of the American people, while the American people adapted to *them*. Like all truly fervid love affairs, this one—we could have guessed—would prove to have a limit. But while it was going strong, "Sputnik" only served as a booster rocket of sorts to the appropriations flowing from Washington and from our state capitals.

---

[1] Clark, Kerr, *Troubled Times for American Higher Education: The 1990's and Beyond* (Albany, N.Y.: State University of New York Press, 1994), pp. 25–26.

Needless to say, few messages are more unwelcome to most academic minds than the notion that they participate in "engines of adaptation." Those inclined to feel indignant when they hear such an assertion might point to the elitist system of higher education that preceded the Second World War, when relatively few Americans could report having had "some college."

But that is a way of saying that a considerably more elitist America, in which only envy could be directed by the majority of Americans at the distant privileges of the "lucky few," needed its schools of higher education to be considerably different places than they became later in the twentieth century. In the 1930s, popular humor about "absent-minded professors," and a widespread popular contempt for the intellectual life, helped to determine the culturally defensive, Anglophilic, and often anti-Semitic character of our colleges and universities. (It simultaneously determined, of course, the existence of such geographically demarcated refuges and sanctuaries as Greenwich Village.) American schools of higher education, then as later, were exquisitely adapted to their society, which required of them not merely that they achieve certain levels of accomplishment but also that they serve a certain role as scapegoat—as a reassurance, in effect, that it was perfectly okay, if not preferable, to be *average*.

As additional evidence that our schools of higher education are adaptive engines, only consider their response to the "Sixties rebellion," which was so substantially confined to their campuses, especially those on the East and West Coasts. Even when it was underway, that upheaval was often seen in "representative" terms—as the political expression of a whole generation of young people (what we soon learned to call the Baby Boom Generation) struggling toward what we would today call empowerment. What so many of them had in common, once they had undergone a certain amount of Vietnam-centered orchestration, was indignant feeling. What they also had in common was the fact that so many of them were either college students or college-bound. In short, the assault on our schools of higher education was produced *by the schools themselves*, as they adapted to their newly assigned role: conduits for the indignation of the "thinking class" in an increasingly thoughtful society.

Since the language of apocalypse was very much in the air in the 1960s, tenured professors could have been forgiven the feeling that it was *impossible* to adapt to the kinds of demands now being heard from angry, fist-shaking, often obscenity-flinging adolescents (including, not uncommonly, some of their own teaching assistants and graduate students as well as a sprinkling of junior faculty and an occasional tenured renegade). But adapt is what colleges and universities proceeded to do—a process assisted by the ideologies and demographics of their own younger teachers and their own students. Formerly sacred "requirements" were swiftly reduced or eliminated. The humanities, long considered the peculiar glory of higher education, gave way to curricula much more heavily weighted toward the social and behavioral sciences. The nearest underclass ghetto was suddenly as important as the British Museum or the Uffizi. Courses that would have been regarded as utterly tabu only ten years earlier—courses positively athrob with implicit and explicit political "bias"—were soon being offered to overflows of perfectly official registration.

In similar ways, our schools of higher education adapted to the "rise of business" that followed the Oil Embargo of 1973. Suddenly it seemed obvious to the American people and to their academic mirrors that an MBA degree was the only sensible route to a truly successful career in the national and international economy. At good liberal arts colleges in the 1950s, students proposing to enter the business world were regarded by the campuses' intellectual elite as even further beyond the pale than those planning for careers in "practical" fields like medicine or law. Twenty or thirty years later, they were obviously people with the good sense to be thinking about money. And only ten or fifteen years after that, we witnessed a world of diminishing business enrollments as the connections between academic study and career success became considerably more uncertain.

AND NOW SCHOOLS MUST ADAPT AGAIN—TO A WORLD OF "ACCOUNTABILITY"

So swept up are we by the axioms of "economic threat" that typify the present decade that it may be hard for us to recall the comparable mood of the 1970s.

Back then, runaway inflation was the problem with which schools of higher education struggled to cope. Academic salaries seemed to be falling further and further behind the cost of living. Home mortgages in the 16 percent range seemed destined to rise even higher. And talk had already begun, in our colleges and universities, about the forthcoming "demographic catastrophe"—which never quite happened as predicated.

Looking back across the idyllic postponement represented by the 1980s, we can see that earlier decade as one in which panic often ruled the academic roost and in which fears with regard to "the economy" were nearly as intense as they are today.

But one thing we cannot see when we look back to the 1970s—and that is the level of public suspiciousness and public scrutiny that schools of higher education have learned, in the 1990s, to take for granted. During the Reagan years, and even as schools of higher education recovered from the economic battering of the 1970's, U.S. Secretary of Education Bennett devoted himself to a relentless critique of everything summed up by "Harvard." In 1988, with the publication of *ProfScam: Professors and the Demise of Higher Education*, Charles J. Sykes signaled the onset of a Niagara of books and articles devoted to the alleged shortcomings of the professoriate. ProfScam included a chapter on "The Crucifixion of Teaching" in which Sykes declared "that the academic culture is not merely indifferent to teaching, it is actively hostile to it. In the modern university, no act of good teaching goes unpunished."[2]

If in the prewar world, colleges and universities often represented "ivory towers" in distant isolation, in the period 1988–1994 they came to represent fishbowls subjected to relentless scrutiny by the American public, its omnipresent media, and its political representatives. Few indeed were the newspaper columnists and television commentators who did not utter scathing, ironic, and bitter remarks with respect to the failures of American higher education—and most specifically, its alleged failure to adequately instruct American students. And few better indications were there of the importance higher education had now acquired with relation to the American economy.

Increasingly, these critiques began to influence state legislatures and state governors and their budgetary behaviors toward the public colleges under their jurisdiction. Like the national media, they began to look ever more closely, ever more critically at the actual time spent by faculty members on teaching and advising and at the actual quantity and quality of the research they produced. The question suddenly on everyone's mind was: "Is the college education being delivered worth the price we are

---

[2] Charles J. Sykes, *ProfScam: Professors and the Demise of Higher Education* (Washington, D.C.: Regency Gateway, 1988), p. 54.

paying for it?" And as the unforgiving global economy of the 1990s made its new range of impacts on every single American, this question was even more closely defined: "To what extent is 'college graduate' synonymous with 'employable person'?"

Accountability was the new watchword—in business, in the professions, and, increasingly, in higher education. A salary, the new axiom ran, could no longer be pocketed without an explanation of what the earner had done to deserve it. Where colleges and universities were concerned, the new mood was summed up by U.S. Secretary of Education Richard W. Riley, who addressed the Middle States Association of Colleges and Schools on December 6, 1993 and observed that the American people:

> know the value of education and what your institutions offer. But this rising demand takes place against a backdrop of higher costs, tighter budgets, a troubled student financial aid system, and a growing demand for accountability. . . . I want to talk to you candidly, as a seasoned political observer and friend of education, on the new impatient public mood now sweeping the country: how this new public mood of accountability and desire for higher standards will affect your work, how, ultimately, our efforts to ratchet up the level of quality and excellence at the K–12 level, by its very nature, will eventually—indeed, is already beginning to—put the "spotlight" of reform on you in higher education.[3]

Within a few weeks, Secretary Riley's office clarified the forms that accountability would now be taking in the world of higher education. In a meeting with seventeen college and university presidents, including myself, that took place in his office on January 5, 1994, the Secretary and his most senior associates discussed proposed regulations for academic accreditation, and for a new State Postsecondary Review system, under Part H of the Higher Education Amendments passed by Congress in July of 1992.

Among the documents prepared by the American Council on Education in a background memorandum for the participants in that

---

[3] "Remarks Prepared for U.S. Secretary of Education Richard W. Riley" as released by his office. A few changes in punctuation have been made by the present author.

meeting was a summary of the Standards for Institutional Review by the various State Postsecondary Review Entities (SPREs) to be set up when final regulations are used this year. Included among these standards, in the words of the ACE, are the following:

- The accuracy and availability of catalogs, admissions requirements, course outlines, schedules of tuition and fees, policies regarding course cancellations, and the rules and regulations relating to students.
- Assurance that the institution can assess a student's ability to successfully complete the course of study for which s/he has applied.
- Assurance that the institution maintains and enforces standards relating to academic progress and maintains adequate student and other records.
- "If the stated objectives are to prepare students for employment," the relationship of the tuition and fees to the remuneration that can "reasonably be expected by students who complete the course or program," and the relation of the courses or programs to providing the student with quality training and useful employment in recognized occupations.
- Availability to students of relevant information, including: (a) information relating to market and job availability for students in occupational, professional, or vocational programs; and (b) information regarding the relationship of courses to specific standards necessary for state licensure in specific occupations.
- The success of the "program at the institution," including:

  a. graduation or completion rates, taking into account the length of the program and the selectivity of the institution.
  b. withdrawal rates.
  c. with respect to vocational and professional programs, the rates of placement of the institution's graduates in occupations related to their course of study.
  d. where appropriate, the rates at which the institution's graduates pass licensure examinations; and
  e. other student completion goals, including transfer to another institution of higher education, full-time employment, and military service.[4]

---

[4] Memorandum of the ACE's Division of Governmental Relations to Participants in the January 5, 1994, Meeting with Education Secretary Riley to Discuss Accreditation and State Review of Postsecondary Education, dated January 3, 1994.

As even this selection from the ACE's paraphrase of the proposed regulations makes clear, and though the regulations may undergo some changes before they are issued in final form, the "accountable" school of higher education, be it public or private, will form a virtual antithesis to the college or university of three or four decades ago. Back then, the word "clubby" was often an appropriate adjective where academic life was concerned—not least because so many of the most important decisions were made by senior professors over lunch at the faculty club, or by the president and a few trustees huddled around a good sherry in the former's walnut-paneled office. In contrast, Secretary Riley and his office are interpreting Congress's purpose in passing the Higher Education Amendments as "a flinging-open of the blinds" worthy of Ibsen's *Master Builder*.

Schools of higher education are already required by federal law to make public the crime rates on their campuses and the graduation rates of their athletes. Now, it appears, they will have even fewer secrets indeed from an inquisitive public and its media representatives. In particular— and this is confirmed by the parallel standards that the Department of Education is proposing for our regional accreditation agencies—schools will be required to monitor and to reveal the "job placement rates" of their graduates. They are entering upon a period in which they will be held responsible not only for their procedures but their *products*.[5]

A NEW TRIUMPH IN THE MAKING FOR THE LIBERAL ARTS?

As *The Economist* made clear in the issue which I have extensively quoted, Americans have developed, as their principal objection to the current state of their schools of higher education, what they perceive as a dysfunction in the area of teaching. An unflattering but increasingly common portrait of "typical professors" includes not only the use of teaching assistants as lecturers, sometimes to very large classes, but also unavailability to students outside of class, failure to keep posted office hours, and a pervasive lack of interest in the careers their students will be pursuing after they graduate.

---

[5] "Subsequent to the delivery of this essay, the Department of Education initiative (described on page 73–75) was overtaken by events, making moot the unique challenge it presented. However, the general point illustrated ultimately remains no less pertinent to the national higher education agenda for the 21st Century."

American schools of higher education come in many different varieties,[6] ["You've got your research universities on the one hand," I recently wrote to the editor of this journal, "and your research-*oriented* universities—and your institutions of higher education—and your institutions of further education—and your teaching institutions—and your vocational institutions."] and the question has always been whether the blanket indictments cited in this article fit all of them or even most of them and more than—in most cases—a fraction of their teachers. The large majority of instructors today—those not in the "Nobel Prize class"—have good reason to know that conspicuously poor teaching can damage their careers. Student evaluations form part of their official personnel records. Student-sponsored publications regularly and sometimes ruthlessly evaluate the teaching skills of every instructor on campus. Indeed, the phenomenon of "grade inflation," recently a subject of particularly anguished discussion in this country, may be attributed in good part to the instructorial fear that a bad reputation with students, and classes of reduced size, are bad attributes with which to be saddled in our age of severe economic stress.

My own sense—based, admittedly, on personal and anecdotal evidence, but of a wide-ranging kind—is that we are witnessing a sea-change where alert faculty attitudes are concerned. Once-reflexive distrust of "the administration" is giving way to the understanding that administrators, like faculty members and staff, are all "running scared," and that "we're all in this together." Most of all is this the case because schools of higher education, unlike so many American businesses of the present time, do not positively *glory* in letting people go. Their humanistic inclinations *do* extend to the reluctance with which, when forced to, they contract their payrolls.

The sea change I perceive as taking place at the present time among those on college and university payrolls can also be described as a collective change of consciousness centered on the fact, now broadly understood, that "every bit of it has to be paid for." It resembles the moment in a child's life when he or she suddenly understands that Mommy and/or Daddy work for a living and are as dependent on their paychecks as he or she is on *them*. "The administration," far from being a monolithic entity devoted to waste and obfuscation, consists of very

---

[6] Letter to Stephen R. Graubard dated December 29, 1993.

individual *administrators*, each of whom has good reason to be concerned with the economic viability of the institution as a whole—not the least of those reasons being, where he or she is concerned, the complete absence of tenure.

In other words, American colleges and universities are now in the process of making the transition from an age of "shared governance"—with its implied resentment against governance by administrators—to an age of shared responsibility, in which everyone on the school payroll is driven by the concern for institutional programmatic and fiscal survival.

Does this represent a disillusioning "come-down" for formerly dignified schools in which a smart faculty member had access to all kinds of privileges and perks? That is only the case if we insist on holding onto the vision of a college or university as qualitatively different from profit-making corporations and—in *today's* world, at any rate—efficiency-minded government agencies.

Accountability is more than a fashionable watchword. It is a new national and global ideal, closely related to the triumphant vision of "the agora." And both of these values, in turn, are closely tied to the democratic notion of an emancipated and empowered citizenry. Whether the version of accountability now being entertained by Secretary Riley's office is the one that will prevail is beside the point. Secretary Riley knows that he is on the right track by making the *concept* of accountability into his, and his department's, North Star.

Not too long ago, the fact that *accountability* is derived from the world of finance—from the idea of "keeping accounts"—would have disqualified it from being taken seriously in most academic contexts. "I'm not a bookkeeper," a faculty member might well have declared in a venomous tone. "I deal with the quest for *new knowledge*, and decades or centuries may pass before my contribution can be adequately evaluated." Today, language of that kind is restricted, by fairly common consent, to those on academic rosters who have scored heavily in *the marketplace of ideas*, including the level of that marketplace in which Nobel Prizes and other major rewards are distributed. And today, all too frequently, it is those not engaged in what used to be called "applied" research—those whose research is unlikely to revolutionize our lives within a few years—who need to do some explaining when they attract the attention of funding agencies, tenure and promotion committees, or the media. Even where the quest for new knowledge is concerned, accountability is our new norm and the marketplace our prevailing metaphor.

And what does all of this mean for the liberal arts? Here are a few of the things that it seems to mean—and a few of the things that are likely to happen as our colleges and universities continue to move through their present adaptive phase:

The anti-vocational and deliberately "impractical" sense of the liberal arts is drawing to a close.

In effect, and sometimes in geographical fact, the office of the Vice President for Academic Affairs is drawing closer to the office that houses the Career Center.

Even in the 1970s, after all, as students increasingly faced toward the Mecca of employability, proponents of the liberal arts could sometimes be heard to argue that "in our internationalizing business world, you may find yourself dealing with Europeans who have graduated from Oxford and the Sorbonne—and who take a knowledge of Shakespeare or Renaissance painting for granted. You don't want to be the dope at the cocktail party, do you?" The parallel argument today might place more emphasis on speed, efficiency, and clarity communication as attributes for which the businesses of the 1990s actively hunger. If today's e-mail from Los Angeles to Bangkok includes a truly major boo-boo, tomorrow's *Wall Street Journal* may well take notice.

Older divisions between the liberal arts and the social sciences have been definitively overcome.

Anthropological, sociological, and even economic approaches to the history of art and literature have supplanted "pure aesthetics." And our new synthesis typically uses literature, history, and graphic art as windows into "culture," other windows being cuisine, office design, public transportation, the definition of "an adequate living space," the use being made of information technology, and the length of an "average commute."

It was in the late 1950s and early 1960s that the study of what was then called "popular culture" made its controversial appearance on the academic scene—notably in the writings of Richard Hoggart. Today, no one blinks an eyelash, and many applaud, when a scholar like Richard Slotkin of Wesleyan University studies "the western"—the cowboy novel, the cowboy movie, and omnipresent cowboy fantasies—as the American archetype, played out in foreign as well as domestic policy.

But there is a newer archetype that has even more meaning than "the western" for college and university programs in the liberal arts. An American executive is handed a challenging assignment, distinctly more suited for a sage than a gunfighter: to negotiate, either personally or electronically, with executives or government officials based on another continent and drawn from another culture. What he or she now experiences can be called the ultimate internship. Unlike the business scenario envisioned by the liberal arts proponents of the 1970s, this one may involve not Western Europeans but business persons drawn from several countries in Southeast Asia, or from Turkey, or from Mexico and Peru.

Suddenly, a general "openness" to other cultures, the ability to absorb their internal meaning and consistency and their particular responses to the global business challenges of the present moment, has become a major American business virtue. Undergraduate attentiveness to courses that touch on the Western impact on 19th-century China, to the Ottoman impact on Christian Europe, or to the present-day tensions between northern and southern Mexico, can translate into a "feel" for the linguistic and substantive details of a business offer or a business threat received from Hong Kong, Singapore, Bombay, Peshawar, Prague, or Mexico City.

Far from representing a "betrayal" of the liberal arts, such a recontextualization—one that, among other things, synthesizes the liberal arts with the social sciences—may bring them full circle to where the liberal arts began. In the Middle Ages, after all, the teaching of Latin and the preservation of the Latin Classics was an essentially practical affair, since "literacy" at the time was defined as literacy in Latin. Even the translation into Latin of major Arabic texts, including the Koran, was based on the *usefulness* of those texts when refutations of Islam needed to be undertaken by Western theologians for purposes of conversion. Europe was beginning its long "reach-out" to the world, and Europe's strength, in the competition for international dominance, would prove to be its persistent fascination and involvement with the other cultures of our planet.[7]

---

[7] In his important new book, *Islam and the West* (New York: Oxford University Press, 1993), Bernard Lewis puzzles again and again over the primal mystery: why the West's strong interest in Islam was not reciprocated, except in rudimentary ways, by Islamic societies. Richard Knolles' *General History of the Turks*, published in 1603, had no Turkish equivalent. Had the case been otherwise, the Turks' 1683 siege of Vienna might have had a different outcome!

Students' progress will soon be monitored on a new and expanded basis.

Proper use of information technology should make it possible for a school's faculty and administrators to answer, at each point in the student's undergraduate career, a crucial set of questions: "Would you give him or her a job? If not, why not? And if not, then what should we be doing to improve the likelihood that after graduating from our school this student will be perceived, in our new 'fishbowl' universe, as a credit to rather than a criticism of our pedagogical procedures?"

At earlier points in postwar academic history, when "caving in to vocationalism" was regarded with horror by academic practitioners of the liberal arts, vocationalism was in fact being delightfully practiced. Undergraduates who demonstrated conspicuous talent for the study of Shakespeare, or Homeric Greek, or Sienese painting found graduate fellowships awaiting them at major universities and attractive job offers in the mailbox as they completed their Ph.D.s. College and university departments in liberal arts disciplines adapted with pleasure to a rapidly expanding academic universe supported by government largesse—and the adaptation was, in economic and vocational terms, perfectly realistic. Even nationalism played a role in reinforcing this pattern, since the feeling was widely shared among Americans that "a nation as powerful as our own needs to be an academic power—no matter how abstruse the field of study."

The vocationalism of the present time, the new concern with the employability of our college graduates, because it is driven by so much sharper a set of economic concerns, can actually be seen as a relatively more stimulating force in the liberal arts than the pretensions of the immediate postwar period. Books have already begun to appear, for example, which explain how much less of an economic threat Japan is to us than was assumed as recently as a year ago. The public mood that sponsored a novel like Michael Crichton's *Rising Sun* has swum rapidly into a new perspective. Books and articles will soon be appearing which explore the extent to which traditional images of Japan and the Japanese, including those that were current during the Second World War, may have influenced the thinking of American economists from 1980 to 1993.

As this particular dialogue intensifies, will it be possible to draw a clear line between the "economic," the "cultural," the "literary," and the "artistic" aspects of Japan's role in American psyches?

What awaits our liberal arts disciplines, if only they are able to seize the challenge, is a new globalism that powerfully intersects with the economic anxieties of our undergraduates (including older undergraduates) and their families (including the dependents for whom older undergraduates are so often responsible). An optimal instructor in history or literature or English composition will increasingly be one who pays close attention to *The New York Times* and *The Wall Street Journal* as well as the professional publications in his or her field. Nor will such an instructor shy away from discussing with a student, perhaps after receiving a print-out from the Career Center, the long-term implications of—the employment possibilities affirmed or discouraged by—the work that student is doing in Post-Soviet Russian History, Contemporary Islamic Literature, or the Astlan Movement of the American Southwest.

The instruction of undergraduates in liberal arts subjects will once again become a full-time job.

Of all the criticisms being aimed by Americans at their system of higher education, the ones that have left the deepest dents in its hull are those which denounce professional unavailability. At a time when so many Americans are working at multiple part-time jobs—including so many of those who work as college teachers—Tuesday–Thursday teaching schedules, including modest office hours, increasingly look appropriate only for those faculty members who are truly in the "Nobel Prize class."

Not to be minimized in this context, is the impact of information technology. Clark Kerr may be right when he predicts that "the new electronic technology may continue to advance modestly in the conduct of administration and research, but very slowly in teaching."[8] What this observation ignores, however, is the administrative character that a teacher's contacts with students take on once advising and career-related functions are seen as essential to the instructorial role. The mere fact that handwritten or word-processed materials can be faxed from a student's dormitory room to a faculty member's office or home—and back again—is in the process of altering our notions of "the typical academic schedule." The steadily growing emphasis on *portable* electronic equipment—including the commonly envisioned keyboard-fax-modem-

---

[8] Kerr, *op. cit.*, p. 8.

telephone combination—has given the very idea of "being out of touch" an archaic look. And the speed with which students can now electronically "visit" a library catalog, as well as the growing use of the Internet to swiftly obtain information from the ends of the earth, is pervasively "upping the pace" of academic life, including all aspects of teaching and learning. As they seek to envision their future, and the future of the society so many of them are devoted to studying, academicians might profit from contemplating the visions of pace and accessibility that pervade Michael Crichton's most recent novel, *Disclosure*.

The hiring, scheduling, and promotion of teachers in the liberal arts will increasingly favor candidates who are tuned to, and not dismayed by, a world of this kind. In turn, schools whose faculty members are able to achieve "continuity of contact"—particularly with their students, but also with their departments and their colleagues—will have little to fear when accountability-time rolls around. Their appearances and their realities will be characterized by what our inquisitive world now values most, which is openness to inspection, the conviction that one has nothing to hide.

PREDICTABLE ANXIETIES

If adaptation were an easy process, a number of once-prominent institutions and modes of human organization would never have vanished off the face of the earth. But when it comes to adapting, colleges and universities have one major advantage: they are *already* being subsidized by their societies in order to study the world around them, including the origins, self-perceptions, and supportive myths of that world. Moreover, there is a good deal of evidence to support the idea that their adaptation to the new world of the 1990s is well underway. The regulations proposed by Secretary Riley's office, though dismaying in a number of ways, will not come as a complete shock. And those regulations, like the article from *The Economist,* with which I began this article, will themselves give the process of adaptation a helpful boost.

In the United States, more than in any other industrialized nation, colleges and universities play a very special role as social and economic "lubricants." An observer from some other galaxy would be struck by their protean quality, which is able to incorporate—as guest lecturers and as topics for discussion—even their bitterest critics. Not the least of their unspoken assignments is a quasi-allegorical one, which is to serve an emblematic role as expressions of what the society is *currently* all about. And what American society is all about in the mid-1990s is the quest for responsibility, for accountable personalities and institutions that can speak openly about their decisions and behaviors. Answering the moral pressure of such a society, in schools made up, after all, of fallible and very human beings, is and will be an anxious process. But can we imagine a better world for the reinvigoration of the liberal arts?

And now for the good news, which is that adaptation has already begun. Reading their daily newspapers, faculty members and administrators at all levels have come to see themselves as among those privileged to continue the uphill struggle for public acceptance. Less and less often does one hear a note of indignation with regard to the fact that "the Golden Years are past."

Chapter 5

::

Rethinking Administrative Structures

Jillinda Kidwell, **Coopers & Lybrand** *and*
David O'Brien, **Stanford University School of Medicine**

::

For well over two centuries, including the most recent forty years of extraordinary post-World War II growth, the basic academic structure of U.S. higher education has not changed. The academy continues to function, with notable success, through a loosely coupled system of individual faculty interacting within intellectual disciplines organized into programs, divisions, departments, schools, colleges, and universities.

The administrative support structures that serve the academy, however, have changed considerably. Notably absent for most of American academic history, they have emerged in the last twenty years as a significant component of colleges and universities, and an increasingly expensive portion of the institutional budget.

Administrative support services have traditionally centered around faculty activities. As these activities have expanded in recent years, driven in part by academic freedom principles that allow enormous latitude over the direction and content of scholarly pursuits, the administrative support resources allocated to them have grown as well. Increasingly large administrative support groups are attached to and controlled by individual faculty and program groups, divisional and departmental chairs, and school deans. Similar structures have evolved around the offices of university president, provost, and vice presidents.

Over time the bureaucratic expansion has resulted in a diffusion of responsibility, authority, and workload throughout the institution. Contributing to the problem is the tension that exists between central and departmental control groups. Since accountability for the institution is ultimately held centrally while most resource and spending authority has been delegated to faculty in the departments, a complicated series of checks and balances has been put into place to guard against system abuses. These checks and balances, seemingly reasonable at first glance, require faculty (or their representatives) to forge their way up through several layers of administrative oversight to secure successive approvals for desired actions.

Process Navigators versus Central Specialists

The accretion of these labyrinthine processes has gradually led to changes in the administrative structures of both academic departments and central offices. In the departments, faculty secretaries of old have given rise to a proliferation of administrative assistants, or process navigators, on whom faculty rely to move paperwork efficiently through the system. Whether processing a research proposal submission, a travel reimbursement, a simple equipment purchase, or a personnel requisition, the road to administrative approval begins at the door of the process navigator, who provides the only safe, reliable, and responsive way through the maze. Without their intervention, disappointing delays can be expected. In the hiring process, for example, the navigator knows who to contact them to either get the posting date retroactively dated, thereby cutting nearly two weeks off the posting time, or even better, how to waive posting altogether. Process navigators are ferociously loyal to their faculty and will go to whatever lengths are necessary to shepherd paperwork through the system and keep frustrations and system inefficiencies away from their employers. As they strive to achieve their goals, process navigators burn departmental resources at a healthy rate creating tools such as shadow systems, logs, and databases that track the progress of paperwork and access up-to-date management information.

Expending resources just as fast are the *central specialists* whom process navigators frequently encounter in their paths. Central specialists are the experts that work on behalf of the central administration to control, for example, sponsored projects, travel reimbursements, capital equipment, and personnel. They are in many ways the departmental navigators' counterparts. Their numbers have increased over time as well, and their loyalties to their supervisors are just as fierce. Central specialists work hard to protect the university's control within their areas of expertise and consequently, paperwork that reaches them is often directed back to faculty for additional information or corrections. The process thus often appears to the departmental process navigator to be a case of one step backward for every two steps forward until a final outcome is achieved.

Attempts in recent years to reduce the high costs associated with this model of academic support—process navigators versus central specialists—have been ineffective. One reason is that the efforts have come mostly from central university administrators, who "own" a relatively small portion—typically only 20 percent—of the activities that comprise the total end-to-end administrative process. Remaining activities are controlled by the dean's office staff, academic departmental chairs, and individual faculty members.

The Case for Change

Reducing the costs built into this complicated administrative hierarchy is one of the most significant challenges facing higher education today. It has become imperative to achieve. Past administrative growth was fueled in large part by a fortuitous combination of factors including a robust national economy, high interest rates, strong federal investments in cost-reimbursed basic research, and a steadily expanding and cost-reimbursed national health-care program. In the mid-1980s, however, higher education planners began to raise concerns about the potential dampening of these growth factors. Preceding decades of growth had produced a rapidly expanding community of academics. Now they could be forced to compete aggressively for ever smaller pieces of the higher education pie. As interest rates began to fall, so did expendable earnings from endowments. Tolerance for double-digit inflation in tuitions and fees also declined. More recently federal research support has flattened (in constant-dollar spending) and become refocused on direct costs at the expense of institutional overhead cost reimbursements. State and local funding has also been constrained, and tax code changes have diminished philanthropic support. And shifts from cost-reimbursed to capitated health-care systems have eroded a significant source of support to institutions that deliver health-care services.

The economic picture for higher education in the 1990s differs in almost every way from past decades. The administrative organization that developed in those years was largely unplanned and has remained largely unchallenged. It is characterized by processes so interwoven into the fabric of academic departmental structure as to be nearly inseparable. The new economic realities that confront higher education require a serious rethinking of the way that work is done, the way it is organized, and the systems needed to support the academic enterprise. To successfully develop a new business model appropriate to the economics of the future, this rethinking needs to question the academic departmental base as the underlying condition for the delivery of administrative support services.

REENGINEERING THE ORGANIZATION

Several years ago, administrators responded to the cost crisis as if it were a temporary problem. Financial resources, they felt, would ultimately return to previous levels and enable them to spring forward to even higher levels of administrative support. The early response to budget imbalances was to implement across-the-board cost-cutting measures or freeze administrative budgets. These approaches balanced budgets temporarily but did little to provide long-term relief. They produced unsatisfactory results because administrative work did not go away. Instead, the remaining reduced staff did more work with fewer resources. Some forward-thinking institutions implemented innovative strategies in response to the cost crisis such as total quality management (TQM) initiatives, but their results were mostly incremental. To achieve the systemic changes needed, higher education must take more dramatic action.

As evidence mounts that the cost crisis is long term and structural in nature, more institutions are finally seeking ways to initiate radical organizational restructuring. To accomplish change of this magnitude, colleges and universities need to question the underlying assumptions regarding the structure of their administrative tasks. The outcome of this questioning should lead to organizational restructuring, management delayering, employee empowerment, and a culture that is less bureaucratic. Those who embark on this road need to be prepared to restructure their business services and administrative operations to the point of even giving up certain long-established responsibilities, taking on new responsibilities, and collaborating in heretofore unheard of ways (e.g., "hub" structures to provide administrative services to a group of three or more departments).

The Corporate Experience

Many corporations have faced and overcome the challenges currently confronting higher education. An army of writers has declared the death of corporate bureaucracy. Traditional American corporate structures—complex organizations with hierarchical chains of command, narrowly defined roles and responsibilities, numerous layers of management, and excessive division of labor—are considered artifacts of a bygone era, increasingly irrelevant in today's changing business environment. According to Michael Hammer and James Champy in their landmark book *Reengineering the Corporation*:

> Advanced technologies, the disappearance of boundaries between national markets, and the altered expectations of customers who now have more choices than ever before have combined to make the goals, methods, and basic organizing principles of the classical American corporation sadly obsolete. Renewing their competitive capabilities isn't an issue of getting people in these companies to work harder, but of learning to work differently. This means that companies and their employees must unlearn many of the principles and techniques that brought them success for so long.[1]

D. Quinn Mills considers traditional hierarchy to be a threat to our economic survival in his book *The Rebirth of the Corporation*:

> The traditional hierarchical structure of our companies is more than just a system that has outlived its usefulness—it is a clear and present danger to the economic welfare of all of us. . . . Perhaps in the past companies needed to be organized as if they were old-time military units. People were poorly educated and required precise direction. They were reluctant to work and

---

[1] Michael Hammer and James Champy, *Reengineering the Corporation: A Manifesto for Business Revolution* (New York: HarperCollins, 1993), 11.

poorly self-disciplined, so they needed close supervision. Because communications were slow and information difficult to obtain, many people were needed to collect information and prepare reports for top executives. The result was a pyramid of supervisory managers who kept business humming and rewarded themselves with good salaries and high status.[2]

Today's corporate reengineers are taking apart hierarchical business models and developing process-oriented organizations in their stead. Customers, who were previously viewed as downstream receivers of company output, are being focused on at the beginning of the business process and now help define product requirements. Organizational boundaries are blurring as companies begin to share broader responsibilities for output with their suppliers.

As workers focus more on customer needs and are empowered to design effective systems in response, their need for traditional supervision wanes. Narrow bands of specialization vanish as staff become responsible for both the overall performance of a process and its end results, delivered to customers. Employees organize as self-managed process teams; they no longer rely on constant middle-manager directives to inform their activities. As old functional departments dissolve, managers become more like coaches, and hierarchies flatten. Ultimately, the need for process navigators disappears as reengineered processes allow those in line positions to manage work effectively by themselves and deliver services as dramatically reduced costs.

In their book *The End of Bureaucracy and the Rise of the Intelligent Organization*, Gifford and Elizabeth Pinchot describe employees that:

> put their heads together to milk opportunities, co-create products and services, find and solve problems. They "get in over their heads" and help each other emerge with stronger skills and a bit more wisdom. Employees run their areas like small businesses, service their internal and external customers with care and work with others across the organization to make

---

[2] Daniel Quinn Mills, *Rebirth of the Corporation* (New York: John Wiley, 1991), 13–14.

sure the whole system is going well. Everyone, not just the people at the top, is exercising his or her intelligence and responsibility at work.[3]

Applying Reengineering to Higher Education

The empowered workforce that the Pinchots describe sounds almost too good to be true and may seem difficult to envision in higher education. The academy's elaborate system of controls, checks, and balances does not lend itself readily to such a transformation. Higher education's heavy reliance on multiple levels of approvals, numerous signatures, etc., tends to create processes that are a series of handoffs and black holes. Tracking transactions becomes a significant activity in its own right as staff spend substantial time developing systems to aid them in responding to paperwork queries.

For higher education to reap the full benefits of reengineering, the changes in its systems that eliminate built-in process inefficiencies will need to be accompanied by changes in its culture—a culture of mistrust and control where checkers check checkers and "going around the system" is rewarded. To facilitate the transition to a more trusting environment, new technologies can be applied which provide workers with up-to-date decision-making information. Expert systems that instantaneously step through complicated decision trees enable faculty and staff to take immediate direct action instead of paging through manuals and policy books, tasking process navigators, or consulting central specialists for answers.

Higher education must also change its underlying management values. Classification systems need to become less restrictive, and new methods of feedback and performance evaluation need to be developed for people working in self-directed teams. Accountability should be clear and direct; system abusers should suffer punitive consequences and exceptional workers should be rewarded.

THE REENGINEERING PROCESS: AN OVERVIEW

Reengineered organizations are customer-driven, results-focused, and performance-based. The new organization shifts its focus from a

---

[3] Gifford Pinchot and Elizabeth Pinchot, The End of Bureaucrocy & the Rise of the Intelligent Corporation (San Francisco: Berrett-Koehler Publishers, 1993), 5.

functional, or vertical, orientation to a process, or horizontal, view that cuts across functional units. Processes previously fragmented across several departments are restructured into a cohesive whole that provides services to end-customers more cost-effectively.

Reengineering therefore begins by identifying an organization's processes. A process is a series of linked activities in which an input is transformed into an output and a tangible product is delivered to an external customer. Unfortunately, rigorous application of Adam Smith's division of labor principles has led to hierarchical structures with excessive departmentalization, making it difficult to identify a process from beginning to end. The beginning of a process often has no connection to its end. Because most processes are characterized by handoffs among numerous departments and obscured by complicated work steps, much time must be spent at the start simply defining an organization's existing processes. To do this, an organization's outputs and external customers must be identified. In higher education, attaining agreement on who these customers are is often an arduous task. Many faculty and administrators even balk at using the word *customer*.

The reluctance to accept the existence of external customers and the rejection of the idea that an institution produces measurable outputs and products are obstacles to higher education's reengineering efforts. For example, a reengineering team that fails to define its customers correctly will by default fail to define the university's core processes correctly. Reengineering teams that abdicate their responsibility and do not own up to the customer definition task will be hampered in their reengineering efforts. For example, a team that agrees to an amorphous customer definition such as "the state's taxpayers" or "the general public," will find it difficult to define the product it delivers to the customer or the process that creates the product. Unless accurate definitions of customers and outputs are achieved, defining processes and creating an institutional process map are nearly impossible.

Evaluating and Fixing Processes

Once a process is defined, it can be evaluated according to how critical it is to an institution's mission. A process's degree of saliency indicates its value. In deciding what to reengineer, an institution can use process saliency to help gauge how much effort should go into a particular process redesign. Heaviest investments should go to improve an institution's most value-creating processes. The cost to redesign a process should never exceed its benefit to the institution.

Processes can be categorized as *core* or *non-core* depending on whether they support an institution's mission-critical activities or not.

Core processes can be further segmented into:

- *Identity processes*—Processes that affect what an institution stands for, "who" it is, and how customers think about it. The institution's vision, mission, values, priorities, and sense of shared culture all relate to its identity processes. These processes must be consciously maintained as assets and strategically positioned to avoid becoming liabilities.
- *Priority processes*—Processes that comprise important elements of an institution's business and directly link to and support identity processes. Priority processes make a material difference in the ability of an institution to achieve a leadership position in its identity processes.

Non-core processes can be divided into:

- *Background processes*—Processes that are a part of what an institution does but do not directly support its identity processes. As such, background processes should not consume undue time, resources, or attention, nor divert critical resources away from the institution's identity and priority processes. Reengineering efforts often center around ways to implement background processes adequately at the lowest possible cost since they often harbor the most waste.
- *Mandated processes*—Processes that are performed only because the government or other external agencies impose them. These processes rarely add economic value. Care should be taken to minimize the effort and expense expended on these processes and yet comply adequately with regulation.[4]

Not all processes should be reengineered. Reengineering teams should challenge the status quo by asking whether certain processes might be eliminated. Financial stringency dictates that institutions cut back, if not cut out, "nice to have" but nonessential services. Activities and

---

[4] These terms were coined by Ellen M. Knapp of Coopers & Lybrand L.L.P.

services deemed essential but non-core should be considered for outsourcing. Functions such as bookstores and dining services are obvious candidates for outsourcing. Not so obvious candidates include physical plant services, payroll, human resources, audit, computing, security, and back office processing. *Business Week* describes the growing outsourcing trend in business:

> Hundreds of big companies have outsourced non-core operations: Continental Bank Corp. has contracted its legal, audit, cafeteria, and mailroom operations to outside companies. In September, American Airlines Inc. announced it would do the same with customer service jobs at 30 airports. . . . Outsourcing can work wonders for the bottom line: So-called contingent workers get pay comparable to full-time staff's, but without benefits that typically add 40% to labor costs. A contingent workforce, too, is more flexible: When business sags, the temps go first. Blue Cross/Blue Shield of Rhode Island cut its workforce by 40% over five years without laying off a single full timer.[5]

If an activity or service cannot be eliminated or outsourced, can it be made more cost-effective, customer-responsive, and efficient? For example, can redundant administrative work taking place in a multitude of departments be "in-sourced" to a single process team that provides end-to-end processing thereby increasing timeliness and service delivery? Can the process be completely automated using advanced technology? Can the organizational model be re-structured by creating a single customer service desk for students that handles registration, housing, library privileges, dining, financial aid, and other essential student services? It is possible to design a hybrid process in which the central organization sets standards and provides necessary infrastructure while devolving control to the end-user?

There are numerous types of process solutions; one size does not fit all. Each institution will make unique decisions based on its mission, values, and the degree of supporting technology that exists.

---

[5] *Business Week* "Special Report: Rethinking Work," October 17, 1994, p. 85.

Higher Education's Process Map

Before processes can be redesigned, they need to be understood. One of the key tools of reengineering is the creation of a high-level business process map. According to Hammer and Champy:

> Process maps don't require months of work to construct; several weeks is the norm. But this task does induce headaches, because it requires people to think across the organizational grain. It's not a picture of the organization, which is what people are used to seeing and drawing, but a depiction of the work that is being done. When it's finished, the process map should not surprise anyone. In fact, people may wonder why drawing it took as long as it did, since the finished map will be so easy to understand, even obvious. "Of course," people should say, "that's just a model of what we do around here."[6]

To create the map, it is necessary to identify the outputs created by the institution's core processes and define the customers to whom these outputs are delivered. The map by definition does not show departments but rather shows how work flows through the organization. Because processes have been obscured by organizational structures, employees often have a difficult time creating their first process map. The first step is to ignore department, college, or divisional reporting relationships and think about the processes that define the organization.

Most colleges and universities are able to distill their identity and priority processes into five to ten core processes. The following five core processes represent a typical distillation:

- Create and sustain the intellectual community of the institution through strategic planning and resource allocation
- Manage faculty resources
- Generate new knowledge
- Educate students
- Provide community services

The relationship among these processes is diagrammed in the high-level process map shown in Figure 1.

---

[6] *Reengineering the Corporation*, p. 121.

Figure 1. Higher Education's Process Map

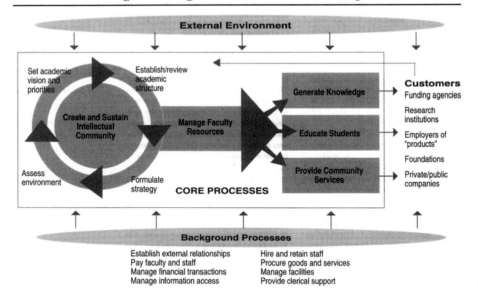

The way in which an institution implements these processes helps to establish its reputation in the academic community. For example, one of higher education's core processes is its ability to create and sustain a dynamic and compelling intellectual community. The establishment of that community—accomplished by strategic planning and budget setting subprocesses—is one of the primary assets that enables an institution to attract and retain faculty. Subsequently, these faculty members generate new knowledge through research, educate students, and provide community services. Their teaching, research, and service activities produce distinct and measurable products (outputs) to the institution's customers including for example, the business community that employs its students, federal agencies that fund its research, patients who receive medical care, and community members who use its services. At the end of the intellectual community building process, customer feedback—satisfaction levels, changing customer needs, etc.—informs strategic planning and the process begins anew.

Each process on the high-level process map is the parent to a group of related subprocesses that can also be mapped (Figure 2). These detailed subprocess maps can be extended to identify the personnel needed in each department to execute specific subprocess tasks.

Figure 2. Subprocess Map for Knowledge Generation Process

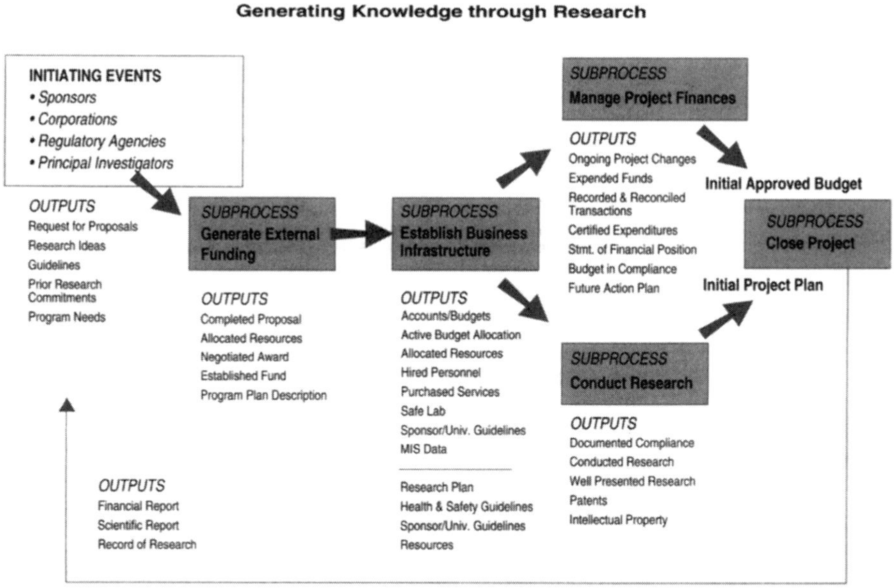

Generating Knowledge through Research

The high-level process map showing how processes link to and support the institution provides a framework in which to discuss transforming higher education. Simply stated, it depicts the way work is done. In reengineering, institutions will structure processes that ignore traditional hierarchical boundaries and follow these natural, horizontal workflows.

This philosophy of reengineering formed the basis for discussion recently at Stanford University's School of Medicine. The school's experience reflects what is happening throughout higher education today. It experienced phenomenal growth followed by a significant cost crisis. In 1994 a representative group of its staff began to explore ways to respond to the deepening crisis. Traditional cost-saving strategies were evaluated and rejected. The group concluded that radically restructuring administrative support was the most effective action the school could take.

THE STANFORD UNIVERSITY SCHOOL OF MEDICINE EXPERIENCE

In 1962 the Stanford University School of Medicine reported a total consolidated budget of just under $7.1 million. At that time, the school consisted of 118 faculty members supported by 72 administrative staff. Of these staff, nearly 80 percent were departmental and faculty secretaries. Consequently, less than $500,000 was budgeted for administrative staff throughout the school. This amounted to less than 6 percent of the school's total spending and just 4 percent of all departmental spending. The school's entire central administration consisted of three administrative deans and seven support staff.

By 1992, thirty years later, although the school's faculty size had jumped by nearly 400 percent, to 571, its consolidated budget had grown to $231.2 million (a constant dollar increase of over 600 percent). This expanded enterprise was supported with a 1,000 percent increase in administrative staff, now totaling 835 people in 76 different job types, and a 1700 percent (constant dollar) increase in administrative costs. Secretaries (although budgeted within five different job grades) comprised just 20 percent of the administrative workforce. The predominant departmental job groups were now administrative assistants, office assistants, and accountants. Administrative costs now consumed nearly 15 percent of all school spending and over 25 percent of departmental spending. The rise in faculty process navigators had produced a constant-dollar increase of over 300 percent in departmental administrative costs per faculty member.

At the same time, Stanford, along with several other universities, was in the midst of an attack by the federal government for cost accounting methods used to set sponsored research indirect cost rates. The government unexpectedly and retroactively reduced Stanford's effective indirect cost rate for 1990 by over 30 percent, which at the School of Medicine resulted in an immediate and sustained loss of some $12 million in budgeted unrestricted annual income—nearly 20 percent of general funds support.

Although it had recently undertaken a downsizing effort in response to more subtle changes in its financial forecasts, the school's administration responded to the lost indirect cost recoveries with an immediate 5 percent reduction in central administrative staff, followed shortly by an across-the-board 7 percent reduction in general funds allocated to academic departments, a one-time salary freeze, reductions in planned faculty billet increases, and an additional 6 percent reduction in central administrative units. Combined with other adjustments in the school's financial plans and reserves management, the school was left with a continuing base budget shortfall of about $2 million by 1993.

In response, the school's dean convened a group of departmental and central administrators to study administrative costs and advise him on options for further reducing costs in order to balance the budget. In addition to continuing conventional downsizing approaches and exploring opportunities for TQM applications, the study included an assessment of business process reengineering approaches to administrative restructuring at the school. The study's results have helped school academic and administrative leaders to better understand the limitations of the school's prevailing business model and to identify the risks and opportunities of pursuing a new and different approach.

The School's Process Map

The hierarchy of activities and taxonomy of administrative processes presented earlier provided a unifying framework for studying the School of Medicine's administrative costs and structure. The study began with the development of a process map of the school's activities. Traditional administrative inventories usually ask the question, "What do we do?" and tend to produce effort measures within the existing organizational chart. A high-level process-based view of the school was produced by repeatedly asking the question, "To what end do we do what we do?" and yielded a unique view of the critical outputs of the school. The school's data indicated that between 525 and 590 full-time equivalents (FTEs) of staff effort was expended in administrative tasks. These FTEs cost the school between $30 million and $35 million. Despite the relative importance of the priority processes to the success of the school's academic mission, nearly three fourths of the FTEs and two thirds of the staff costs were attributable to the administration of background processes. In Figure 3 these processes are depicted on a process map to indicate how each process links to and supports other processes and to show the output to the school customers. It also shows the costs (in millions of dollars) of the school's administrative activities.

Perceptions of the School's Processes

Focus groups representing the recipients (customers) of the school's administrative efforts indicated a high degree of customer dissatisfaction with the performance of nearly all of the school's administrative processes. The faculty's confidence in the administration's value, ability,

Figure 3. Stanford School of Medicine's Process Map

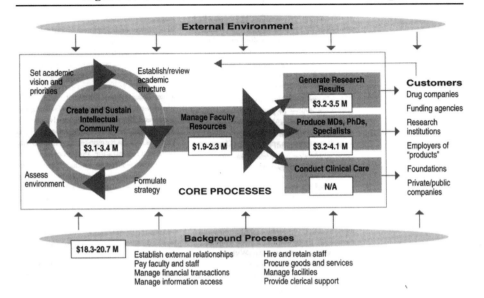

and willingness to get things done decreased in direct correlation to the distance at which the process activity took place from their own offices. From the faculty's perspective, the most valuable participant in the process was their local administrator. The only way to get anything done was to rely on their local administrator—the process navigator—as a go-between, bridging the gulf between their academic program needs and an unfathomable and unresponsive administrative bureaucracy.

Local administrators clearly viewed their faculty as their customers and expressed their frustrations with this go-between role and the extraordinary effort expended in meeting the demands of faculty. Faculty and their local administrators expressed a distrust of the motives and abilities of central medical school administration and suggested that if they could simply be left to do their jobs, things would run just fine. Local administrators evidenced a particular pride in the private shadow systems they each developed to support their work in ways that the official university systems could not. They frequently measured their successes by how well they could shortcut the university's processes, often by knowing key persons who controlled critical steps in the process. "Process busting" was a skill highly valued by their faculty supervisors and an activity from which they derived much professional pride.

Focus groups representing the providers of central medical school administrative services generally saw the university or external agencies as their customers. They expressed great frustrations with the attitudes and capabilities of the faculty and their local administrators. They felt that if the faculty and staff would just learn the university's policies and procedures, the jobs in the medical school's central offices would be made much easier. While these central administrators acknowledged their effect on the pace of administration and the frustrations expressed by the local staff as a result of their prolonged reviews and frequent returns of work, they consistently rated the quality of their work as "high." This is an understandable difference in perception from the faculty view since central administrators did not see the faculty and local administrators as their customers.

In all the focus groups, individuals expressed a clear understanding of their specific jobs. They knew in infinite detail their particular pieces of processes that often began and ended elsewhere in the institution. They did not, however, express a sense of responsibility for the overall performance of any process. From a process view, the School of Medicine's administration consisted of a vast array of individuals all working very hard at their assigned tasks, with little or no understanding of their contributory role within the larger processes that were critical to the school's success.

Implications of Administrative Fragmentation

Detailed staff effort data were collected and analyzed by the school's reengineering team. They helped express the school's administrative effort and costs in relation to the processes involved. The data indicated a great deal of process fragmentation within the school, which reinforced the focus group findings. Within an organizational unit (i.e., a division or department) many different staff members were involved in various phases of a process. Also, staff from across all levels of the organization participated in a process.

Not surprisingly, the data indicated a similarly high degree of *position* fragmentation within the processes. Position fragmentation is a measure of the number of individuals required to yield a full FTE of administrative effort within a process area. In most cases, the lower the ratio, the better.

Figure 4 shows a sample process fragmentation table. At the School of Medicine, position fragmentation ratios ranged from a low of 1.75 (recruiting M.D. and Ph.D. students) to a high of 10.37 (research project closeout). Across all processes the school averaged a fragmentation ratio of 1.57. Within priority processes, however, the ratios were higher: 2.66 (educating students), 3.42 (establishing vision and recruiting and retaining faculty), and 3.81 (generating research results).

These ratios were a concern for two reasons. First, they indicated that the average administrator was spending only one fourth to one third of his or her time on priority processes critical to the school's success. Second, these ratios implied that the school would have trouble sustaining its downsizing efforts. Traditional approaches to the budget crisis were not going to work. Across-the-board cost cuts reduced costs short term but did not fundamentally eliminate administrative work. Similarly,

Figure 4. Sample Process Fragmentation Table

Process	Indivs.[a]	FTE[b]	Frag. Ratio[c]	Avg. %[d]
PRIORITY				
Recruit/retain faculty	94	19.2	4.9	20
Generate external funds	89	17.1	5.2	19
Establish infrastructure	24	3.4	7.1	14
Manage project finances	102	25.5	4.0	25
Hire/retain postdoctoral candidates	43	11.6	3.7	25
BACKGROUND				
Close project finances	31	3.0	10.4	10
Hire/retain staff	74	19.5	3.8	25
Procure goods	291	41.0	7.1	14
Manage facilities	155	23.0	6.8	15
Manage access to information	79	37.6	2.1	48

[a] Number of individual staff members who indicated they had participated in the process.

[b] The number of individual staff involved expressed as full-time equivalents (FTE), based on the percentage of time spent by each individual on the process.

[c] Fragmentation ratio. The ratio of individuals to FTEs, it indicates the degree of fragmentation in the process, i.e., the process is structured such that no person spends most of his or her time on it. The higher the ratio, the more fragmented the process.

[d] Average percent. The ratio of FTEs to individuals multiplied by 100, it indicates the average percentage of time an individual spends on the process.

incremental process improvements (TQM) improved performance some-what but were impossible to translate into reduced staff costs. Radical workflow improvements in at least three or four processes are required to achieve staff reductions. The school's data revealed a highly fragmented work environment where efforts to improve workflow were hindered by the fact that such improvements usually affected only a portion of a person's job.

It became increasingly apparent that without dramatic changes in workflow and organization, the school would not be able to achieve the level of savings it sorely needed. The fragmentation data indicated that without larger-scale organizational changes, neither traditional downsizing nor TQM techniques appeared to offer real opportunities for the school to achieve and sustain its administrative cost saving.

A New Organizational Construct

Faced with low customer satisfaction, high costs, and high fragmentation, the medical school began to explore the potential impact of business process reengineering on its staffing, costs, and organization. Fortuitously, the university was already engaged in several campuswide reengineering initiatives of its own including redesigns of the processes by which staff and faculty buy and pay for goods and services and generate and submit research proposals. The university reengineering teams had produced conceptual models that identified radical new processes to supplant the existing ones. The medical school staff used these models to explore ways in which the new university processes might facilitate the school's own administrative restructuring. Concurrently, new financial client software had just become available that allowed the school's departments to directly access central database servers and eliminate the need for shadow systems, time-consuming reconciliation processes, and costly maintenance personnel.

Incorporating the effects of the university's proposed redesigns on the school's processes, the school's study team produced an administrative organizational model that:

- uncouples the administrative from the academic
- organizes administrative units around priority processes that focus on supporting individual faculty

- organizes administrative units around background processes that focus on delivering minimally invasive service and support to priority processes by maintaining reliable and responsive institutional systems
- staffs administrative units with fewer people more focused on specific process areas and operating with much greater authority to support desired products and outputs

At the heart of this model is the creation of several process teams to support the school's identity processes. For example, the school envisions a team of research process managers (RPMs) who support the complete research process from pre- to post-award. RPMs would have signature authority and the power to cut through bureaucracy but would report to a process owner, the associate dean for research, and be accountable to customers (the faculty) for submitting proposals promptly and supporting research fund management. Technology would facilitate the process. Software would provide RPMs with appropriate proposal templates and sophisticated financial management tools. RPMs would have no departmental reporting relationships. They could serve faculty from a number of departments. Decoupling research administration support from the narrow boundaries of the academic department would enable the school to reduce the number of staff members participating in the process by 50 percent. The school envisions developing other process managers to support the recruitment and retention processes for both students and faculty.

The high-level conceptual design of the new organization is presented in Figure 5. The success of the School of Medicine's model depends on Stanford University's continuing campuswide reengineering efforts. The maintenance of large numbers of staff to participate in "broken" university background processes is an expense that the school can no longer afford. The new high-level buy/pay process intends to deliver a process so simple and straightforward that every member of the Stanford community will become a "shopper" and will be able to procure most goods without the help of process navigators or procurement specialists.

The efforts of the school's team to untangle administrative costs from its academic departments provide lessons for other institutions contemplating reengineering. To date most reengineering efforts stop at the door of a school or academic department; little work has been undertaken to realize the results promised by reengineering. The school's

**Figure 5. Proposed Administrative Organization Chart:
Stanford University School of Medicine**

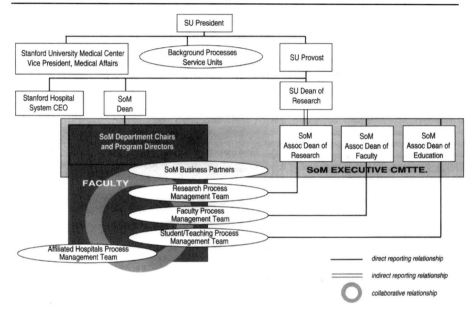

hard look at the structure and organization of the administrative tasks within an academic department indicates that substantial change is possible. In general, radical change is possible in higher education if institutions are bold in their approach to redesign and do not set limits or boundaries on the process.

CONCLUSIONS

Is it actually possible for higher education to achieve the results promised by reengineering? Does corporate restructuring have any relevance for academia? Is a radically different organization model possible?

The answers to these questions are: Yes, yes, and yes. Radical change is possible. This transformation will not be an easy task, nor will it happen overnight. In fact, the road to a transformed institution can be treacherous. It requires both stamina and a dedication to goals that may at times seems impossible to attain in higher education. The road to transformation begins by requiring that college and university administrators establish a healthy skepticism regarding the status quo and be ready to let go of traditional approaches. Essential ingredients for success will be the desire, inclination, and ability of people from disparate functions across the institution to work together cohesively to develop a new business model.

Therein lies the most difficult challenge: Designing a new model is easy; achieving consensus around it is hard. Most colleges and universities are characterized by a highly decentralized, boundary-sensitive environment in which responsibility centers focus on maximizing their own benefits rather than taking a "What's best for the institution?" view. Most institutions also seem to lack an adequate "tiebreaking" mechanism that would facilitate tough decision-making.

However, restructuring will force an institution's leadership to wrestle with important issues regarding the role and responsibilities of its campuswide, university-provided functions, school-based central administrative functions, and departmentally-based administrative functions. In short, by reengineering, an institution's leadership will be answering the fundamental underlying question: What is the most appropriate business model for a complex, decentralized organization?

The answer will ultimately be one of organizational design: To what extent is the institution willing to "go horizontal," moving from a functionally oriented organization to a process-based one? How empowered will employees be to operate in teams and make decisions about their processes without going through organizational hierarchies? Failure to address these difficult questions consciously throughout the organizational change process may thwart the success of any attempt to change. However, confronting these questions directly and aggressively can enable an institution to reengineer itself successfully, saving substantial costs and positioning itself strategically for the future.

Chapter 6

:::

Simulating the Academy
Toward Understanding Colleges and Universities as Dynamic Systems[1]

Jesse H. Ausubel, **Alfred P. Sloan Foundation,**
Robert Herman, **University of Texas at Austin,**
William F. Massy, **Stanford Forum for Higher Education Futures,**
Sally V. Massy, **Jackson Hole Higher Education Group**

:::

Colleges and universities are complex and arcane enterprises. They create and archive fundamental and pragmatic knowledge. They educate our young in preparation for adult life and society's various endeavors. They interpret and critique culture and influence our world views. We expect these institutions to be all things to all people: generator of inventions for industry, spur for regional economic development, surrogate home for the young, guarantor of good jobs and high incomes, professional developer of those in mid-career, entertainer on Saturday afternoons, equalizer of social opportunity, and political refuge. As important as colleges and universities are to us, however, they are not well understood at a systems level even by those who live and work inside them.

This lack of understanding mattered less when the academy was held in high esteem and resources flowed to it at rates sufficient to maintain internal

---

[1] This paper was motivated in part by a session on simulation and gaming led by John Hiles of Thinking Tools, Inc. at the November 1995 Stanford Forum for Higher Education Futures in Annapolis, Maryland.

107

stability. But times have changed. The gleam of the ivory tower has dulled. A growing number of critics now believe that while educational services are central to America's successful future, existing colleges and universities are failing to adequately manage their affairs, adapt to changing student needs, and exploit technological possibilities. Internal strife, from heightened competition for scarce resources among a heterogeneous mix of campus constituencies, makes governance increasingly difficult. Tools that can provide leaders both inside and outside the academy with a greater shared insight and understanding of our institutions of higher learning as dynamic systems are needed. This paper proposes one such tool.

The Need

Overemphasizing higher education's importance in America is hard. It is a huge and influential enterprise. Roughly half of all young people enter a higher education institution. About 15 million students currently enroll. Faculty number about 90,000. In 1995, spending totaled close to $180 billion.

As a result of mounting difficulties in raising revenues, rising expectations for the role of universities in social and economic development, technologies that extend the ways in which education can be delivered, and shifts in student demographics and graduate labor markets, many academic leaders are seeking to move beyond incremental change and embark on more fundamental restructuring. Debate has in fact spilled beyond the borders of academe into the contents of best-selling books, lawsuits, and other areas on such issues as:

- the fundamental roles of the university (mission, vision)
- the relative emphasis on research, quality of teaching
- the need, quality, and character of basic research
- the appropriateness of applied research on campus
- faculty responsibility and behavior
- (excessive) management and (lack of) leadership
- costs, especially tuition and overhead rates
- the rationale for and length of time to the doctoral degree
- employment terms for the academic workforce
- curriculum content and knowledge structure
- elitism, social stratification, and diversity
- academic standards (e.g., admission policies, attrition rates, grade inflation, sports)
- the rise of foreign student population and links to foreign firms

The desirable response from higher education seems clear enough. From community colleges to research universities, they should raise productivity, modernize administrative and support services, and improve accountability while preserving autonomy. Upon identifying priorities, they should recast incentives and allocate resources accordingly. But how to go about achieving this response is less clear. A major obstacle is that *key stakeholders appear not to recognize or accept facts about how colleges and universities work.* They do not view the institution as a system or internalize the linkages between cause and effect. The resulting gaps in knowledge and credibility form major barriers to experimentation and reform. For example, seemingly logical proposals to close marginal departments and redeploy their faculty are vigorously fought. Conversely, incentive programs for early retirement are readily accepted even though they may generate unintended and undesired consequences (e.g., those who leave may be among the institution's more productive faculty since they are more likely to have compelling career alternatives).

A large share of the problem owes to the fact that universities are complex, both to understand and to manage. Considering their functions and interactions with government, industry, and society in general, we can hardly be surprised. Universities are systems with many independent parts and interactive processes. Outcomes frequently depend on powerful but obscure second-order effects. One example is how the expansion of graduate education created a market for low-cost provision of labor for research and teaching, which now strongly influences the size of graduate programs and admissions, including the admissions of foreign students.

Some of the complexity in managing the system stems from lack of agreement or clarity among the various stakeholders about purposes, measures of performance, and productivity. Furthermore, the professional workforce and relatively flat organizational structure limit the exercise of direct management control, leaving institutional leaders to reconcile conflicting objectives as each stakeholder presses his or her own agenda. Stakeholders often attend only to their own values and needs, not stopping to see their institution in broad perspective. The decision-making process becomes volatile when emotionally charged issues such as tenure, academic freedom, and diversity are perceived to be at stake. Choices ultimately made may not be congruent with the institution's long-run interest.

Most academic leaders come to their jobs lacking deep experience about economic and management matters. Intelligence and motivation can offset their inexperience to some extent, but organizational complexity limits the offset. The difficulty of achieving a comprehensive view also applies to trustees, faculty, staff, students, and others involved in university decision making. Trustees are typically grounded in a business or professional field but often lack recent firsthand exposure to the higher education environment. Faculty rarely view their institution holistically, and the same is true for students, alumni, and other stakeholders.

Higher education needs innovative devices that help institutional leaders focus their thoughts and then communicate with stakeholders without appearing manipulative or quickly raising defense mechanisms. Traditional devices such as conferences, commissions, and editorials help, but people rarely internalize complex scenarios by passively receiving information. A program to understand the college/university as a (complex) system, synthesized in a leadership strategy simulation game, can provide people at several levels with an opportunity to deepen their understanding of how colleges and universities work, motivating and engaging them without imposing the difficulties and risks that come with real life.

People concerned with higher education need to understand the decision-making process of the major actors—administration, faculty, students, and other internal and external stakeholders—and how these processes interact. Modeling the behavior of various subsystems within the university, their interactions, and the influence of external forces upon them can contribute to such an understanding. The parts of the system to be analyzed and modeled in detail will depend on what are considered the most important issues. Since controllability of the entire system is of paramount concern, priority would attach to building a model of the behavior of the entire complex system—yielding an intriguing, though necessarily rough, view of the whole.

A Leadership Strategy Game: "SimU"

The development of a college/university simulator, or "SimU," would draw on three streams of activity: (a) management education games now widely used in management education (e.g., MIT and Carnegie Mellon distribute corporate management games popular in business schools); (b) special-purpose simulations developed to meet educational objectives in enterprises of various kinds (e.g., military battlefield simulations, nuclear power plant operations simulations); and (c) more purposely entertaining simulation games developed for a broader commercial market. Games such as SimEarth and SimCity (both developed by Maxis Software, the latter with sales of 2.5 million units) have proved to enlighten as well as amuse. Although formal evaluation of their effectiveness is hard to obtain, the enthusiastic adoption in school and university courses suggests their educational value. More explicitly serious simulations in this genre such as SimHealth (developed by Thinking Tools, Inc., to explore the reorganization of the US health-care system implied by the Clinton health-care reform proposals) have also had reasonable commercial success (sales of tens of thousands of units).

The games use continuous computation and constantly changing color graphics as well as sound to sustain user interest. Individual players "play against the model." SimCity, for example, confronts a single player with zoning, infrastructure, transport, security, and fiscal issues played out over a sweep of time sufficient for long-term effects to become apparent. Efforts at developing multi user on-line simulation games (e.g., the Internet-based "President '96" and "Reinventing America," developed by Crossover Technologies under grants from the Markle Foundation to simulate the political and policymaking processes) are also now attracting considerable interest.

The authors believe that existing research and data are sufficient to build a simulation, both educational and entertaining, that will allow users to grapple with issues such as:

- strategic positioning of the institution
- academic performance and faculty morale
- administrative and support service performance and staff morale
- incentives and rewards
- goals and perceptions of students, parents, donors, research sponsors, community members, employers, and government
- comparative performance with respect to similar institutions
- tuition, financial aid, and overhead rates
- financial performance, including capital assets and liabilities (e.g., endowment, physical assets, and deferred liabilities)

The target market for such a simulation would be, broadly, anyone with an interest in how colleges and universities work as systems and, more specifically:

- higher education administrators

- faculty, especially those in leadership roles (e.g., department chairs)
- trustees
- educational analysts, writers, and policymakers
- students of higher education, and in general
- alumni and interested public

How SimU Might Work

One of the biggest challenges in building the simulation will be to develop a successful user interface. It should be highly graphical and easy to understand and use. It should draw users to a depth sufficient for meaningful learning while at the same time maintaining interest, pace, and playability. Users report playing SimCity many times to experience its wide variety of different scenarios, exogenous events, and patterns of consequences. SimU should elicit a similar degree of interest.

SimU might open by inviting the user (you) to choose among institutional types and control. Do you want to lead a private research university, a public comprehensive, a private liberal arts college? In what year would you like to begin play? What would you like to name it? You might choose to "grow your own" generic institution or load one of a handful of pre-scripted scenarios that present a specific institution in the throes of a specific dilemma based on actual case studies. The scenarios would define "victory goals" that you must achieve to "win." (In regular game mode, you will be free to define what success means yourself as you hone your own goals over time.) Versions of the game might be developed that would allow tailoring to match more closely your specific real-life institution (e.g., through the loading of custom data sets).

Play might open with a panoramic view of the campus: a map with icons representing various organizational units and functions that then segues to a close-up of "Old Main," your administrative headquarters. Double-clicking on it reveals the interior of an office (yours) complete with desk, file drawers, computer (for e-mail and information display), perhaps a door to a conference room in which meetings could be conducted and a window overlooking the campus that reveals significant changes in various aspects of the campus environment (e.g., dilapidated buildings if maintenance is deferred for too long, fewer students milling around if enrollment declines substantially, hostile faculty if you have not recently appeased them). You, by the way, are the president/senior administrator of this institution and have been blessed (burdened?) with an uncannily high degree of omnipotence.

Clickable icons to the side of the screen could represent schools and departments, offices for managing various functions (e.g., admissions, fund-raising, buildings and grounds department), athletic facilities, dormitories, etc. Clicking on an icon would provide information about and/or encounters with the people or activity—analogous to searching out reports and management by walking around. Figure 1 provides a sampling of the kinds of activities and reports that might be included in the simulation.

Figure 1. Sample Activities, Decisions, and Reports

Operating Units
Academic departments
Student services and student life
Admissions and financial aid
Institutional advancement
Alumni relations and
   public affairs
Libraries
Information technology support
Intercollegiate athletics
Finance and administration
Plant operations
   and maintenance
Dormitories and food service

Financial Decisions and Reports
Operating and capital budgets
Tuition rate and financial
   aid policy
Research overhead rate
Sources and uses of
   operating funds
Faculty and staff salaries
Faculty early retirement buyouts
Endowment asset allocation and
   investment return

Debt issuance and retirement
Balance sheet
Operating surplus/deficit

Other Actions and Reports
Admissions selectivity and yield
Enrollment by degree level
   and major
Attainment rates and
   times to degree
Course offerings
Teaching method mix
Course availability
Class size distributions
Teaching loads
Sponsored research volume
Publications record
Faculty awards, prizes, etc.
Popular prestige ratings
Academic prestige ratings
Faculty age distributions
Faculty hiring retention
Staff additions and layoffs
Staff turnover rates

At this point you might proceed in one of two ways. You might provide a set of presidential goals: in effect, a "platform" that calls out the priority you attach to various stakeholders and outcomes. Alternatively, you might begin by playing with the goals programmed into your chosen scenario. These goals would influence certain aspects of simulated behavior. Moreover, they would provide the institutional performance benchmarks needed to define what it means to "win" the game. Alternatively, you might choose to simply explore the simulated world. Rather than trying to "win," you would be occupied with observing the intuitive and sometimes surprisingly counterintuitive, consequences of various inputs you and others (driven by the underlying game engine) make over time.

Semester by semester, time passes as you observe (and seek to modify) outcomes like faculty gains and losses, shifts in applicant pool and graduation rates, growth or decline in externally sponsored research, crumbling buildings and infrastructure, and accreting or eroding financial health. Conditions permitting, you might raise or borrow money and construct new facilities. You may at any time review data in your office or by walking around, calling meetings, or changing certain policies. (Nothing will happen at the interface while you are engaged in one of these activities, but computations will continue in the background.)

You might visit a particular department and perhaps try to influence faculty behavior: e.g., numbers and types of courses, teaching loads, submission of proposals for sponsored research, involvement with students outside of class. Such efforts might or might not be successful, depending on the institution's incentive-reward environment (which would stem in part from your own prior decisions) and other circumstances. Even if successful, they might exact a price in faculty morale—however, the opportunity to exert influence would allow you to seek changes at the academic working level that might otherwise appear out of reach.

Three kinds of preprogrammed events punctuate the passage of time:

- Scheduled events marking milestones or providing periodic information for which no response is required: e.g., quarterly and fiscal-year financial reports, key athletic outcomes, admission of the next freshman class, commencement. Simulated time continues.
- Scheduled events for which a response is required: e.g., submission of the annual tuition recommendation, the operating

budget, and the capital budget; and the Board's annual presidential performance evaluation and your acceptance or disagreement with it. Simulated time halts while you prepare the budget or react to the performance evaluation.
- Unscheduled events arising exogenously or because of some condition within the simulation: e.g., a stock-market crash, a dean or professor pleads a case or airs a grievance, a Faculty Senate action or student protest, a fire or a safety problem. Simulated time may continue or halt depending on the event.

By combining these events with the user-initiated ones, the SimU program should be able to provide a simulation that is sufficiently rich to realistically represent the essentials of university leadership and capture user interest. Most of the databases needed to specify the model already exist, and a growing number of research findings are available. Indeed, pulling together the information needed to build the model will be a valuable exercise in its own right. A companion handbook and strategy guide could provide background, help focus play, and draw out lessons contained in the simulation.

SimU Actors

We have already described how you (as institutional leader) might interact with the SimU simulation. But in a university, the administration's word is not exactly law. Much of what happens in SimU would result from the actions of various constituencies—simulated actors and stakeholders that operate inside or outside the university. Your actions would influence constituency behavior, but not control it.

A list of potential constituencies follows. Some are depicted as individuals while others represent aggregations of individuals. Some would appear in the simulations for all institutional types, others would apply to one or two types only. At this point we do not know how practical it will be to include all the following constituencies in the game's initial version.

Internal constituencies

- *The governing board* might provide financial oversight and offer evaluations of presidential performance

- *School deans* might be simulated as independent agents who have independent objectives and set policies
- *Faculty* in each department might be simulated as a set of cohorts with age-rank characteristics and probabilities for promotion, departure, and retirement
- *Department chairs* might decide about course offerings, teaching loads, and research emphasis—in effect, representing the aggregate view of departmental faculty
- *The faculty senate* might represent the view of the faculty taken as a whole
- *Students* might be simulated in terms of admission cohorts, degree levels, and majors, each with course-taking, graduation rate, satisfaction, and similar characteristics
- *The student senate* might represent aggregate student views
- *Non-academic operating units*—e.g., support services, administration, operations and maintenance—might be described by production functions relating the quality and quanity of outputs to budget allocations (see Figure 1 for a more complete list)
- *Staff*—the nonfaculty workforce—might be portrayed as a small number of groups, e.g., professional and administrative, clerical, operations and maintenance, whose numbers would grow or ebb according to budget allocations; staff morale and efficiency might depend on workload in relation to numbers, and on compensation level

External constituencies

- *Prospective students* might be simulated in terms of application and matriculation rates by market segment; "market research" data might be used to convey attitudes and predict behavior
- *Research sponsors* might be simulated on a discipline-by-discipline basis, with each discipline characterized by the level of total funding and the intensity of competition
- *Alumni and potential donors* might be simulated according to their interest in one or another department or in the whole institution; gift-giving might depend on department/institution performance and prestige
- *The media* might be simulated as a single constituency, with media actions being illustrated with newspaper clippings or television stories

- *Public opinion* also might be simulated as a single constituency; public opinion might drive *regulatory decisions, and influence state funding decisions in game sessions dealing with public institutions*

Exogenous factors also might affect SimU's fortunes. Economy-wide inflation and family income growth might drive up cost and mediate the effect of tuition increases on admissions yield and public opinion. Demographics might affect student demand. Governmental funding decisions might drive sponsored research and, for public institutions, state appropriations. A natural disaster might disrupt campus operations. Technological change might restructure cost functions and engender new competition that challenges market shares in education or research. Presidential actions throughout the simulation would determine how well the institution weathers the storms and captures the opportunities.

Issues to be Addressed

SimU would address at least four kinds of issues. The interaction of player decisions with data and response functions built into the model would determine how a college or university evolves and whether the president's goals are achieved. Gaining insights about these issues and learning to analyze them in systems terms would constitute one of SimU's most important benefits. The issues include:

1. *Capital investment vs. spending for current operations (spending versus saving):* policies governing financial capital (endowment, reserves), physical capital (facilities, equipment), and spending for operations. Most institutions bias decisions toward spending for current purposes, especially salaries. The simulation would address the consequences of such imbalances.

2. *Operating budget allocations:* decisions to spend more on one field or activity than another; determination of cross-subsidies between fields and activities. Spending on certain fields may be seen as more or less consistent with the school's mission, and fields will vary in their ability to generate enrollments and sponsored research dollars. Spending on academic support services may improve educational and research quality and competitiveness, institutional-support investments (e.g. G&A and O&M) may improve infrastructure and efficiency, institutional-advancement investments may increase giving levels, and so on.

3. *Transactions with customers and stakeholders:* student applications, admissions, and yields; sponsored research finding; gift acquisition; and, for public institutions, state appropriations. Outcomes may be affected by quality and prestige, net prices (e.g., tuition minus average financial aid, the effective research overhead rate), and "marketing" expenditures (e.g., for admissions and institutional advancement), as well as uncontrollable factors.

4. *Academic department actions:* which produce the institution's instruction and research outputs. The range of simulated action might include: the profile of courses as represented by teaching method mix (lectures, seminars, labs), course level, and degree of specialization; faculty teaching loads; and the degree of emphasis placed on research. Considerable attention would be placed on departmental actions because such actions constitute the central focus of academic production.

Success Criteria and Performance Measures

Both game designers and players will have to address basic questions dealing with the university's or college's fundamental mission. Should the mission stress the preservation and transmission of knowledge (teaching) or the generation of knowledge (research)? Should the mission cater to the few or virtually everybody (the elite or the mainstream)? Should the institution focus its mission or should it try to serve a broad set of constituencies?

The SimU simulation would be rich enough to permit a large number of performance measures to be reported, but it would not dictate what players should pay attention to. Indeed, much of the data available as a byproduct of the behavioral simulations would not be displayed unless the player searches it out by clicking on the appropriate icons. While certain success criteria would be defined—either by the player or as part of the chosen scenario—the player will retain a great deal of latitude.

Much of SimU's value will come from discussions about values, performance measures, and the functions programmed into the game. These discussions would be stimulated but not brought to closure by the software and supporting data. The players themselves would have to supply the missing pieces, but the game would supply two crucial elements:

- First, the game would provide a specific set of stimuli for discussion—a context within which to explore one's own values and understandings and, depending on the circumstances, to compare them to those of one's colleagues.
- Second, the game would enforce the disciplines of *conservation* and *causality*. Money allocated to one priority is not available for another. Actions and failures to act have consequences that must be considered when trying to satisfy one or another constituency. All constituencies cannot be satisfied to the full extent of their desires, especially when exogenous forces infringe on the institution's market power or freedom of action.

These are important lessons in their own right, and their application in the context of discussions about values would add yet another important benefit. Without consideration of conservation and causality, discussions about values become unbounded, and the university is urged once again to be all things to all people.

Conclusion

The motivation for using SimU is to understand better how a university works. What performance measures should be considered? How do decisions made by the administration, the faculty, and other agents affect the performance measures? Why can't the university simultaneously maximize the agendas of all its stakeholders? Some participants will challenge the theories used in the simulation, but the very act of challenging requires the formation of an alternative hypothesis—which can be analyzed and compared with assumptions and data used in the model. SimU also should be fun to play, since learning depends on engagement and engagement will be stimulated and sustained if the activity is intrinsically interesting.

Faculty, staff, students, and trustees must develop more coherent and realistic perspectives about their institutions. Working with a simulation game can build experience and broaden perspectives. Gaming can help all stakeholders understand issues at the level of the institution—and from viewpoints of other stakeholders—and see the issues through less parochial eyes. Even experienced managers find that playing a sophisticated game expands their horizons and motivates broader discussion of management issues.

Ultimately, we would hope that development of SimU would bring three benefits:

1. *New knowledge:* advances in fundamental understanding of how a university functions will come from facing for the first time the challenge of modeling the whole of a university.
2. *Education of a broad group of stakeholders:* given a reasonably sound simulator, a rather large number of stakeholders, numbering in the tens of thousands, may enhance significantly their understanding of the university as a system by "playing the game."
3. *Development of new management tools for universities:* while SimU would be generic, it could prove the concept of university simulators and stimulate the subsequent development of more detailed, realistic simulators appropriate for specific institutions or classes of institutions.

The authors understand the difficulty of considering the university as a complex system. But because complexity lies at the heart of the university's current problems, we feel it is important to address the issue head-on. Even the limited models that are practical using today's knowledge can begin to capture the dynamics and the interactions of the parts. At a minimum, they can help organize the data that will be needed to simulate a university in finer grain, and they will lead to better definition of parameters, variables, and outcomes. But the real payoff—achievable, we believe, with today's technology—will be to move higher education's many constituencies toward more shared understanding of how the academy works.

Chapter 7

::

Budget Equilibrium Model

Jon C. Strauss, **Worcester Polytechnic Institute**

::

O ver the years, college and university business officers have spent enormous amounts of time trying to educate others that, while budgets can be balanced by bringing expenses into line with available revenues, they do not stay balanced unless the relative growth rates are balanced as well. This issue has become particularly relevant in recent years as the rapidly increasing costs of financial aid and competitive pressures on price have limited the rates of net revenue growth. This paper presents a very simple algebraic model developed at Worcester Polytechnic Institute to help explain these phenomena. Interestingly, this model facilitates the determination of necessary conditions for achieving budget equilibrium and even offers some suggestions for restructuring expenses to assure budget equilibrium.

SITUATION

During the fall of 1994 as we were considering once again the challenges of balancing the WPI budget for the FY 1995–96 year, we were lamenting (as we seemed to do every year!) the difficulty of our situation. It was bad enough that we had a fundamental imbalance between how rapidly we could increase the overall revenue net of financial aid (estimated at 2 percent) and how rapidly our various colleagues wanted to increase these program expenses to cover inflation (estimated at a minimum of 3 percent), but our colleagues also wanted to add new net expenses to the base expense budget for *program improvements* of at least 1 percent. To top it all off, the various program officers pointed out that commitments that had been and/or were being made during the 1994–95 year would cause the base budget for the next year to be out of balance by some 2.4 percent even before considering inflation and other program improvements.

Some argued, not surprisingly, as they had in years previous, that the obvious answer was to forego salary increases and cut back on maintenance. But, as many have learned the hard way, such strategies are temporizing at best. Deferred maintenance must be avoided in program as well as plant. Accordingly, we focused our efforts on programs and on explaining the budget tradeoffs to our different constituencies.

While we had attempted to use various budget models in prior years to explain the incongruity of this situation to all concerned, the fact that the situation again was repeated, and apparently more pronounced, suggested the need for better conceptual tools. Given the quantitative bent of our various constituents, it seemed reasonable to try to capture this situation in a simple dynamic model to clarify, explain, and, perhaps, demonstrate the necessary conditions for achieving budget equilibrium. This model turns out to be a simple case of one of the budget projection models in Hopkins and Massy.[1] The resulting model may also be used to consider the effects of restructuring program activities to shift variable expenses to categories with lower growth rates.

REVENUE/EXPENSE MODEL

Consider a very simple dynamic representation of revenue and expense and the conditions for equilibrium.

Revenue

$$R = R_0(1 + r_1\delta)$$

Where: R is the operating revenue projected for time δ from all sources net of financial aid expense, R_0 is this year's base revenue net of financial aid expenses adjusted for all known program changes, but not

---

[1] D.S.P. Hopkins, and William F. Massy, *Planning Models for Colleges and Universities*, Stanford University Press, 1981.

rate changes, and r_1 is the estimated relative growth rate for the time period δ (nominally one year).

In September of 1994, the best estimates for R_0 and r_1 at WPI were, respectively, 54.5 ($54,457,000, but the additional digits are not necessary in this equation) and 0.02.

Expense

$$E = P + N + F + I$$

Where: E is the operating expense projected for time δ, P is the personnel program expense, including benefits, N is the nonpersonnel, inflation-driven, program expense, F is the fixed expense (debt service, depreciation, contingency, etc.), and I is the desired program improvement expense.

Now:

$$P = p_0 P_0 (1 + p_1 \delta)$$
$$N = n_0 N_0 (1 + n_1 \delta)$$
$$I = (p_0 P_0 + n_0 N_0) i \delta$$

Where: P_0 is the currently committed personnel expense base for next year, p_0 is the reduction factor necessary for balance, p_1 is the relative growth rate for time period δ, N_0 is the currently committed nonpersonnel expense base for next year, n_0 is the reduction factor necessary for balance, n_1 is the relative growth rate for time period δ, and i is the desired additional relative program improvement for time periods (typically $.01 \leq i \leq .03$).

In September of 1994 at WPI the best estimates for P_0, N_0, and F were, respectively, 36.4, 13.3, and 6.1.

Budget Balance

The conventional approach to balancing the budget for next year ($\delta = 1$) is to determine p_0 and n_0 such that:

$$R = E \big|_{\delta=1} \text{ (Volume Balance)}$$

This condition yields:

$$R_0 (1 + r_1) = p_0 P_0 (1 + p_1 + i) + n_0 N_0 (1 + n_1 + i) + F$$

for budget balance.

This approach requires annual program reductions if the growth rates of revenue and expenses are not equal.

Equilibrium

Another approach is to consider volume and rate conditions for budget equilibrium. Necessary conditions for the projected budget to be in balance for next year ($\delta = 1$) are determined by:

First, balance revenue and expense:

$$R = E\big|_{\delta=1} \text{ (Volume Balance)}$$

and then balance the time rates of change (first derivatives) of revenue and expense:

$$\frac{dR}{d\delta} = \frac{dE}{d\delta}\bigg|_{\delta=1} \text{ (Rate Balance)}$$

(and, of course, to preserve equilibrium, everyone would have to agree not to make any commitments to increase P_0, N_0, or F for the next year that weren't already captured in the I term).

These two conditions yield:

$$R_0 = p_0 P_0 + n_0 N_0 + F$$
$$R_0 r_1 = p_0 P_0 (p_1 + i) + n_0 N_0 (n_1 + i)$$

at equilibrium.

CASES

There are several interesting cases worthy of exploration:

Case 0: Adjust Volume Coefficients for Balance

The simplest budget balance case is to reduce the variable program expense components proportionately to balance only volume.
At $\delta = 1$ and with $p_0 = n_0$:

$$p_0 = \frac{R_0(1+r_1)-F}{P_0(1+p_1+i) + N_0(1+n_1+i)}$$

For the given WPI data and with r_1, p_1, n_1, and I, respectively, of 0.02, 0.03, 0.03, and 0.01, p_0 = .9575.

Successive application of this logic yields the "sawtooth" budget process (Figure 1).

Case 1: Adjust Volume and Rate Coefficients for Equilibrium

The simplest equilibrium case is to reduce the variable program expense components (P and N) proportionately to balance both volume and rate.

Consider: $p_0 = n_0$ $p_1 = n_1$

At equilibrium: $$p_0 = \frac{R_0 - F}{(P_0 + N_0)}$$

$$p_1 = \frac{R_0 r_1}{p_0(P_0 + N_0)} - i$$

For the given WPI data, p_0 = .974 and p_1 = .0255 −i

Thus, for these conditions, equilibrium would be achieved (and maintained!) with a 2.6 percent reduction in base program expense and by limiting the future relative growth rate from inflation to 2.25 percent less program improvement. Experience suggests that it is far more difficult to limit growth rate than to reduce expense, which is probably why most colleges and universities only approximate equilibrium through annual expense reductions. As demonstrated in Case 0, for example, if

Figure 1. Revenue and Expense for Budget Balance

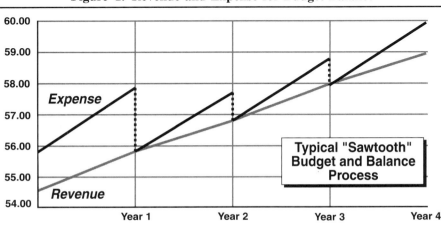

only volume balance was required and p_1 remained at 0.03 with all other things equal, a 4.25 percent reduction in base program expense would be required initially, and successive program reductions of 1.6 percent, 1.5 percent, 1.4 percent, etc., would be required in the following years to reachieve budget balance.

As mentioned earlier, imposing arbitrary limits on expense growth below competition or real program growth will lead to deferred maintenance that will ultimately have to be corrected. There are, however, structural approaches to the problem of achieving budget equilibrium.

Case 2: Shift Variable to Fixed Expense

While the search for productivity gains has been difficult in academe, the new information technology offers promise of replacing variable production costs with fixed. (And thus, bringing the lessons of the industrial revolution to what has heretofore been virtually a cottage industry. To date, however, most of our colleagues in the academy have seen technology more as a way to improve quality than to improve productivity. Increasing competition may change that in the near future! It certainly has for health care!) The concept here is to reduce the average growth rate of expense by shifting expense from high growth-rate variable program expense (P and N) to zero growth-rate fixed expense (F). This model allows us to solve for the shift from variable to fixed expense that would be necessary to achieve (and maintain) budget equilibrium.

Assume $p_0 = n_0$ and determine p_0 and F for equilibrium:

$$p_0 = \frac{R_0 r_1}{(p_1+i)P_0+(n_1+i)N_0}$$

$$F = R_0 - p_0\,(P_0+N)$$

To achieve budget equilibrium then for our original situation requires a p_0 ($=n_0$) of .548 with an allowable F of 27.25. A one-time reduction in variable program expense of over 45 percent and an allowable increase in annual fixed expense of some 350 percent is radical indeed. But, if achievable, it would yield true budget equilibrium with this significant disparity in revenue and variable program expense increase rates.

In practice, such a relatively high budget fraction for fixed expense would not be necessary for any but very rapidly changing technology. A smaller F would allow reductions in prices, higher rates of revenue increase, and rebalancing around a new operating point.

Case 3: Shift Variable Personnel to Nonpersonnel Expense

Another approach to the strategy of lowering the expense growth rate through technology presented in Case 2 is to consider the shift of personnel expenses inflating at 3 percent to nonpersonnel expenses inflating at a blended average rate of 1 percent. Current trends to replace full-time with adjunct faculty and service personnel with contract services would be good examples.

Solving the model equilibrium equations for p_0 and n_0 yields:

$$p_0 = \frac{R_0(r_1 - n_1 - i) + (n_1 + i)F}{P_0(p_1 - n_1)}$$

$$n_0 = \frac{R_0 - F - p_0 P_0}{N_0}$$

With the other WPI data as given, but with $p_1 = .03$ and $n_1 = .01$, $p_0 = .168$ and $n_0 = 3.18$

While few institutions would contemplate reducing personnel expenses by ⅚ and increasing nonpersonnel program expenses by 218 percent, it is nevertheless interesting that such dramatic restructuring would be required for true budget equilibrium under these conditions.

REPRISE

The credibility of this approach to "clarify, explain, and demonstrate" as promised initially is strained by the particularly difficult data of the WPI example. If for example, we adjusted the starting data to reflect initial budget balance with an $R_0 = P_0 + N_0 + F$ (= 55.8) and a less striking rate imbalance of $r_1 = .03$ instead of .02, but still with a 1 percent program improvement factor, the numbers are less formidable.

Case 0: Adjust Volume Coefficients for Balance

$$p_0 = n_0 = .994$$

(Or budget balance with a 1 percent program improvement by repeated program reductions starting with 0.6 percent)

Case 1: Adjust Volume and Rate Coefficients for Equilibrium

$$p_0 = n_0 = 1$$

$$p_1 = n_1 = .0237$$

(Or budget equilibrium with a 1 percent program improvement by limiting base program increases to 2.37 percent)

Case 2: Shift Variable to Fixed Expense

$$p_1 = n_1 = .03$$

yields:

$$p_0 = n_0 = .842$$

$$F = 13.95$$

(Or budget equilibrium with a one time 16 percent reduction in variable program expenses and a permissible increase of 129 percent in fixed expenses.)

Case 3: Shift Variable Personnel to Nonpersonnel Expense

$$p_1 = .03, n_1 = .01$$

yield:

$$p_0 = .934, n_0 = 1.180$$

(Or budget equilibrium with a one time 6.6 percent reduction in personnel expense and a permissible increase of 18 percent in nonpersonnel variable program expense.)

CONCLUSIONS

This model/approach is not magic and certainly does not make the challenge of achieving budget equilibrium in today's competitive environment any easier. It does, however, offer an interesting way to explain why last year's balanced budget won't stay balanced. And, for those institutions brave enough to consider radical restructuring, this approach may help pose and scale some of the alternatives. This model certainly stresses the importance of maintaining revenue growth.

Chapter 8

::

Recasting The Oregon State System

Weldon E. Ihrig, **University of Washington**

::

Since 1991, the Oregon State System of Higher Education (OSSHE) has faced significant cuts in state appropriations. Funding has decreased despite a strong state economy as a result of voter approval for Oregon's Measure 5, a tax repeal initiative patterned after California's Proposition 13. Over the past six years, system support has been trimmed 38 percent.

To compensate initially, programs were cut and tuitions were raised. Enrollment dropped as a result even while projections of future enrollment demand climbed. Figure 1 displays the discontinuity. It compares actual enrollment data since 1980 to system benchmark targets and projected enrollments through 2005, based on state high school graduation growth.

Faced with the constrained access for Oregon students and the certainty that additional state resources would not be forthcoming, we in the system's chancellor's office searched for a structural solution that would effectively address the long-term challenge of reduced state support and the need to teach more students. We concluded that fundamental changes in the relationship between the state and the public higher education system were needed.

We subsequently presented the Oregon legislature with a choice. It could continue to subject the state higher education system to layers of

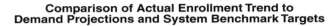

**Figure 1. Oregon State System of Higher Education
Enrollment/Demand Data**

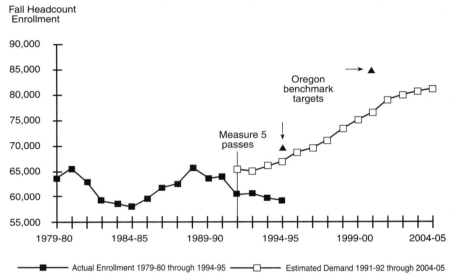

Source: OSSHE Institutional Research Services, August 1995.

governmental bureaucracy that focused on process controls, and we would continue with the downward trend in enrollment. Alternatively, it could allow the higher education system to be converted into a public corporation—removing it from state regulation—and in return, we would agree to teach an additional 2,000 Oregon undergraduate students without any additional state money. Two thousand undergraduate students in exchange for removing bureaucracy—that was the trade-off we proposed.

We thought the trade-off was a great new approach to limited state resources, but it almost died amid political controversy. When the republicans took control of both Oregon's House and Senate in November 1994, however, our proposal fit their agenda and received new life. By July 1995, a key piece of legislation aimed at redefining our relationship with the state was signed into law by the governor. The Higher Education Administrative Efficiency Act (SB271), while not transforming us into a fully independent public corporation, succeeded in establishing the higher education system as a state agency independent from certain state administrative regulations. It shifted authority to determine certain administrative rules and processes from the legislature and state bureaucracy, notably the Department of Administrative Services, to the system's Board of Higher Education. While not embracing all the changes we had envisioned, it did transfer responsibility for purchasing, contracting, personnel, collective bargaining, printing, and travel reimbursements.

At the same time, the act ensures that our system continues to be accountable for its actions through periodic reviews of its budgets, plans, and outcomes by the executive and legislative branches of state government. We can now operate in more innovative, responsive manner since organizational emphasis has shifted from a mindset of mandatory multiple prior approvals to decentralized decision-making distributed down to the department level. The act confers local authority and then provides for increased post-auditing to maintain accountability.

A second piece of legislation (SB2) that was enacted at the same time as the Administrative Efficiency Act did confer public corporation status to a single institution within the system—the Oregon Health Sciences University (OHSU). OHSU is a stand-alone medical university in Portland with a hospital that includes medicine, dentistry, and nursing instruction. As a result of SB2, OHSU is now no longer officially a part of OSSHE (although, from a curriculum perspective, it might still be regarded as a member since it continues to report academic operations to OSSHE's Board of Higher Education). One positive consequence of OHSU's new status, from OSSHE's standpoint, is that the state system is no longer potentially liable for the university's financial shortfalls (e.g., in the case that the university's hospital is unable to compete in the future). From OHSU's standpoint, SB2 provides the flexibility and autonomy from the state necessary to reasonably compete with other health-care concerns in the region. While the university retains the legal protections of the state, its governing board has authority to define all administrative policies.

The new freedoms granted to the state system with the passage of the Administrative Efficiency Act provided us with an exciting opportunity to design our own policies, processes, and procedures. Our challenge was to operate under the new structure efficiently enough to save the money we needed. Figure 2 lists the set of guidelines we developed in anticipation of the Administrative Efficiency Act. The guidelines were formulated even before the legislation was introduced.

Figure 2. OSSHE Guidelines Used In Developing the Administrative Efficiency Act

---

ADMINISTRATIVE EFFICIENCY ACT (SB 271)

- Delegate administrative rules and processes to Board of Higher Education
- Continue accountability to governor/legislature with review of budget, plans, and outcomes
- Allow Board to operate state system in more responsive, innovative, and entrepreneurial manner and streamline business practice
- Change emphasis from preapprovals to postaudits
- Make possible increased undergraduate instruction (2,000 more students) through savings from increased administrative efficiency

We developed them in partnership with the vice presidents from each campus. We used an outside facilitator to guide discussions about how we should operate if we obtained the new authorities requested. To open our thinking, we searched for new terms such as "acquiring things" in lieu of "purchasing." The key was to alter our mindset, focusing on what we would do if we were starting today: how would we approach doing business? The hardest part of the effort was, and continues to be, getting people who have relied on state-established procedures for years to think and do things differently. How do we find ways of breaking out of old modes of thinking?

We have approached this challenge by taking business functions like acquiring things and doing personnel work and asking, what should be the role of (1) the Board of Higher Education, (2) the chancellor's office of the system, and (3) the individual colleges and universities? We considered extending this approach to the roles and responsibilities of the central administrations on the various campuses and at the level of the departments but concluded that campus administrators should have the opportunity to work with their individual departments in determining such roles and areas of delegated responsibility as appropriate for their institution.

Figure 3 shows our thinking relative to acquiring things and contracting for services. It defines the role of the board as developer of an overall policy that says acquiring things should be cost-effective and

**Figure 3. Acquisition and Contracting: Outcomes,
Constraints, and Relationships**

ACQUIRING THINGS AND CONTRACTING FOR SERVICES

Desired outcomes
- best value for the dollar
  - timeliness
  - partnership options
  - exception guidelines
  - access to expertise
    (e.g., technical knowledge)
  - performance and
    vendor data
  - data consistency
  - user friendliness
  - cost-effective processing
    (replace approval levels
    with postauditing)

Constraints
- competitive bidding
- legislative directives
- finance techniques
  (e.g., limits to economies
  of scale and bargaining
  strength)
- public perceptions

Colleges/ Universities

maintain
accountability

define quidelines

delegate responsibility

provide technical support

provide training

manage processes

evaluate
performance

monitor for
compliance

maintain data

approve
exceptions

purchase goods
and services

Chancellor's Office

delegates authority
to institutions

develops model
set of guidelines

approves guidelines

performs post-
auditing

provides legal
support to
institutions

facilitates volume
purchasing

ensures data
consistency

**Board of
Higher
Education**

defines overall
policy

delegates
authority

performs
assessment

competitive. It also presents the board as delegator of authority and assessor of results. The chancellor's office delegates authority further, to the individual campuses, while being careful to avoid replicating the state's bureaucracy in its own organization. Having developed a model set of guidelines and rules for acquiring things that directs institutional behavior, the chancellor's office also approves rules that the campuses develop for themselves within the model guidelines. While the campuses have ample authority delegated to them, the chancellor's office performs postauditing, provides legal support, facilitates volume purchasing when advantageous to the system, and ensures consistency of information. The work of actually acquiring things is done by the colleges and universities (i.e., they have accountability, define their own guidelines, delegate local responsibility, etc).

The Board of Higher Education has developed new rules for acquiring things that are drastically simplified from those of the state bureaucracy's. The board rules are prefaced with a statement of expectations and a code of ethics to help guide employees as they make purchases or enter into contracts of any type.

We have also expanded the use of procurement cards, authorizing their use to purchase amounts of up to $5,000. Departments can go out with a credit card and simply buy what they need. Not only have we streamlined the purchasing of low-cost items, we have also eliminated the accounts payable function for all these small purchases. An information purchase procurement process is used to acquire things that cost between $5,000 and $50,000. A department needs only to obtain three telephone quotes, which they document themselves. For purchases over $50,000 a more formalized process is required, but the campus has freedom to select the process that best fits the need for that purchase. The board rule provides a list of existing competitive processes that may used, but also offers campuses the option to define their own more suitable process as long as it is competitive. Departments don't have to come back for central approval or authorization.

The travel reimbursement process underwent the same review. Figure 4 contains the listing or roles at each level for travel authorization. The campus business managers suggested that we grant per diems for both lodging and meals and eliminate required receipts, and we concurred. Now, once an employee is authorized to travel, he or she is authorized for the per diem rate. If travelers want to eat at McDonald's and stay at luxury hotels or vice versa, they can mix and match the per diem. We

**Figure 4. Travel Authorization and Reimbursement: Outcomes,
Constraints, and Relationships**

AUTHORIZING AND REIMBURSING TRAVEL EXPENSES

Desired Outcomes
- timeliness
- cost-effective processing (reimbursements)
- single contractment evaluations
- report streamlining
- simplified and reasonable reimbursement rates

Constraints
- public perceptions

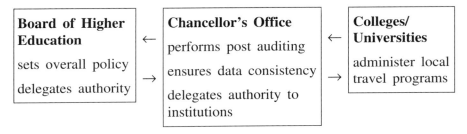

Board of Higher Education		**Chancellor's Office**		**Colleges/ Universities**
sets overall policy	←	performs post auditing	←	administer local travel programs
delegates authority	→	ensures data consistency	→	
		delegates authority to institutions		

don't get involved with the details. If a stay exceeds the federal per diem
rates we use, the traveler personally covers the overage. Again, we don't
get involved. The next step will be to handle the entire travel
authorization process over the computer networks.

We continue to focus our efforts on revamping our business
processes, leveraging our efforts with information technology when
possible to reduce costs and distribute administrative decision-making to
the department level. Out aim is not just to be responsive to cuts in state
support, but to take the lead in discovering innovative ways our available
resources can be stretched to do more of our primary mission, teaching
our students.

DISCUSSION

After his presentation of OSSHE's restructuring at last fall's Stanford
Forum for Higher Education Futures symposium, Ihrig responded to
audience questioning. Excerpts from that conversation follow.

Is this the way you got most or all of the money to restructure your budget problems—just from the acquisition processes—or were other things involved?

Ihrig: Out of the total dollar target in savings, only about 1 percent in savings on the purchases we make is required to achieve our goal, due to our volume of purchases.

So anything that you do in other areas—streamlining work flows and other things—is just gravy on top of that?

Ihrig: We retain whatever we can save beyond the target, which is itself conservative. I was sensitive from the start that a reasonable cost-savings estimate be determined—significant enough to help get the bill through the legislature, but not so high that it would pin our backs to the wall and we would have to struggle to achieve the result.

Your enrollment was going down and demand was going up. What was happening to those students? Where were they going?

Ihrig: We don't know completely. The first wave exited when we did a 38 percent tuition increase in the first year of state cuts. Many of the college students went into community colleges. Community college enrollments in precollege programs went way up, but these students have not returned to pick up on their degrees after two years, as we expected. We think there was a lot of self-selection where students limited their horizon to a two-year technical education and never returned for their four-year degree.

They went into the work force?

Ihrig: Yes, and we think in the long term that this will be a serious concern, when the state brings in a lot of high-tech industries with imported labor.

Oregon students weren't going out of state or anything like that?

Ihrig: There were some going out of state. Utah and Idaho, whose nonresidency fees were pretty low, got some significant increases but not in proportion to the high volumes of students that did not continue. What isn't shown in Figure 1 is that we increased nonresident enrollment by about 40 percent.

Even though fees were doubled or . . . ?

Ihrig: While fees were significantly increased, the number of non-resident enrollments also grew. Oregon's student enrollment declined by 17 percent, so we were really reducing access for the Oregon students by pricing them out of the market due to the reductions in state support.

What was the impact of this new approach on staffing?

Ihrig: We reduced personnel in the chancellor's office 20 percent over this period. Part of our savings stems from not having to pay state assessments for services we no longer use. For example, we had been paying $2 million per biennium to the state for personnel support. Now we do the work ourselves for a million dollars per biennium. I think the real, long-term benefit is going to be people rethinking how to do basic functions rather than relying on the state. It's going to be a cultural change when the campuses start at the department level refocusing their efforts away from central processing and finding new ways to do business.

Did you have to add staff at the campus level?.

Ihrig: No. We set that as a condition. So far there's only been about three new staff member positions systemwide to address the personnel functions.

Some politicians in other state systems are arguing to privatize certain initial areas with the eventual goal to privatize entire systems, but you chose initially to talk about a public corporation and to emphasize that you're not now backing away from being public institutions. Could you comment on the political concerns you had to deal with?

Ihrig: We started out looking at all options. Everything from becoming totally independent to all the alternatives in between. We chose the public corporation as a way to instill a new way of thinking within the academy. That approach would not fly because the legislature saw the public corporation as privatizing, and they wouldn't buy it. They still wanted to have public accountability, so we kept changing the name for what we were proposing. We went through an evolution of name changes, trying to convince them that they still had accountability even without controlling our processes. Rather than assigning a lot of people in the state capital to exercise control, what we're doing is focusing on the real control functions of the legislature: appropriations, expectations, and accountability. We're working with the legislature to focus on the bigger issues. That's why the accountability issue is so important—assisting the legislature in reviewing key factors rather than focusing on the details of our day-to-day business.

Did you get any argument that if you pulled the system out from the state, the state would be negatively impacted?

Ihrig: Yes, we got it heavily and that's where I worried. I never worried that we couldn't sell the legislature. I was always worried that the bureaucracy would kill us in the end; they almost did, and that was their key argument. They wanted us to continue to provide support for small agencies that in light of the budget cuts, we just couldn't afford to do anymore. It's an old argument but fortunately it was losing its cachet; we were lucky in our timing. Also, we had a great board member, the vice president of our board, who could sit in front of the legislators, look them straight in the eye, and say, "Well maybe you need to cut elsewhere in the state, as higher education does more itself." That placed the issue on the table. What has happened since is that the state bureaucracy now looks to us and our experience to learn what it might do to change itself. We've become the model for the rest of the state. It really helps to use your board members to further your cause. They can sit in front of the legislature and tell them where it's really at, something we, as state employees, find sometimes awkward to do because of the different relationship.

You mentioned having secured collective bargaining agreements in the areas where you have more flexibility. Did you mean by that that you now have more flexibility to look at your academic programs and maybe do a little rationalization there?

Ihrig: No, the academic programs are totally outside this authority. We already have complete academic program responsibility. It is the classified employees with whom the state has bargained, for us and for all state agencies, that have now been carved out. We will now bargain directly for our own classified employees and set up our own classification system as we take full responsibility for those employees.

Did the employee union oppose what you were doing?

Ihrig: No. We worked with them ahead of time and guaranteed that we would continue to work with them. Also, the state continued to bargain with them before the new legislation was passed. We're just beginning to bargain with them. It has been somewhat awkward because the Health Sciences University carried over their union which subsequently went on strike. As a term of settlement, OHSU increased staff salaries. We have no resources to duplicate this for our employees. We've tried to focus on the conditions under which people work in lieu of salary increases this biennium. Whether we can continue that approach with what happened at OHSU, I don't know. We made certain deals also with the student lobby groups because they were concerned that the new authority would allow us to raise tuitions indiscriminately. We had to convince them that the state legislature would still have the ability to control increases because its appropriations determined how fast we raise tuitions.

Do you have other states looking at you as a model of what they can do?

Ihrig: We've had a lot of interest from other states. Virginia has tried, and I think they achieved partial success in some of the same areas. The real model on this was done by Jack Blantant in Kentucky in the early 1980s, where they achieved similar results. The key is knowing when the moon and the stars line up in the right place, and you know that it's time to go for it. New York gained a few flexibilities after a commission reviewed their situation, but I think they still have a large number of restrictions. I think a potential danger with our new approach is the possibility that we develop a heavy bureaucracy in the central office, like the University of California or California State systems. We don't have the resources to do that. To avoid this, we have just said that we would continue to streamline the chancellor's staff, even after already cutting personnel by 20 percent. We are also dedicated to changing from the old command/control type environment to a leadership style that sets strategic directions and focuses on accountability. This has been a major challenge. The chancellor's office has brought in a facilitator to help transform it into a learning organization and get people to think differently and in new ways. It is exciting to see what people can come up with when they do begin to change, but it's hard moving them off the dime.

I am aware of another case in which a state system was centralized for the first time and a chancellor's office was put in place over what had previously been a decentralized government structure. Responsibilities for purchasing, payroll processing, and the like were spread out to the institutions so that one institution takes the lead for one function, another institution for another function, and so on. They're hoping to achieve the same thing you did, but they began by centralizing the system a bit.

Ihrig: I think it really shows that you take advantage of whatever your situation is to move from where you are now. That's why it's important to know what the goals are and keep heading toward them. And, to be frank, our proof will be in whether we can increase effective teaching loads to accommodate new students in addition to cutting costs on the administrative side. We believe we can make this a win-win for us. What I'm nervous about is that the state is going to want dollar-for-dollar documentation of our savings rather than allowing the extra thousand students a year to be our accountability factor. Because how do you show savings if you don't purchase something at a lower price? We're still struggling with how to face this challenge.

Contributors

::

Jesse H. Ausubel

Jesse Ausubel is a Program Officer of the Alfred P. Sloan Foundation as well as Director of the Program for the Human Environment at The Rockefeller University in New York City. He leads the programs on "the university as a system and the system of universities" for Sloan. From 1977-1988, Ausubel was associated with the National Academy complex in Washington DC, as a resident fellow of the National Academy of Sciences, then as a staff officer with the National Research Council Board on Atmospheric Sciences and Climate, and from 1983-1988 as Director of Programs for the National Academy of Engineering. Educated at Harvard and Columbia universities, Ausubel has written extensively on both environmental questions and the nature of the academic and research enterprise.

Robert Herman

Robert Herman is L.P. Gilvin Centennial Professor Emeritus in Civil Engineering, and sometime professor of physics, at the University of Texas at Austin. Before assuming his present position in 1979, Herman headed the Department of Theoretical Physics and the Traffic Science Department of the General Motors Research Laboratories. His research has covered a wide range of both theoretical and experimental investigations, including molecular and solid-state physics, high-energy electron scattering, astrophysics and cosmology, and operations research, especially vehicular traffic science and transportation. With Ralph Alpher in 1948, Herman made the first theoretical prediction that the universe should now be filled with a cosmic microwave background radiation, which is key evidence for the validity of the big bang model of the origin of the universe. He holds degrees in physics from City College, New York, and from Princeton University.

Weldon E. Ihrig

Weldon Ihrig was recently appointed Executive Vice President of the University of Washington. Prior to that, he served for six years as Vice

Chancellor for Finance and Administration for the Oregon State System of Higher Education, which includes seven colleges and universities. At Oregon he developed a strategic investment focus and initiatives to enhance other revenue sources during a period of declining state resources. He also oversaw successful installation of a systemwide financial information system as well as the creation of a new relationship with the state to assign more direct authority to the system. Before coming to Oregon, Ihrig was vice president for finance at Ohio State University for nearly twenty years.

William N. Kelley, MD

William Kelley is Executive Vice President of the University of Pennsylvania where his responsibilities include Chief Executive Officer for the Medical Center and Health System, Dean of the School of Medicine, and Robert G. Dunlop Professor of Medicine and Biochemistry and Biophysics. He has led extensive program and financial planning that has culminated in long-term plans on education, research and health services, a comprehensive financial plan, a long-term site and facility plan. Previously, Kelley served as Chairman of the Department of Internal Medicine and Professor of Biological Chemistry at the University of Michigan. Earlier, at the Duke University Medical Center, he was Professor of Medicine and Chief of the Division of Rheumatic and Genetic Diseases. Over the years, Kelley has played an important personal role in research, patient care, and teaching. He continues to be a principal investigator on several NIH and other research projects. In 1993, he received the National Medical Research Award from the National Health Council. He was elected Fellow of the American Academy of Arts and Sciences in 1994, and received the Robert H. Williams Award from the Association of Professors of Medicine in 1995.

Jillinda Jonker Kidwell

Jill Kidwell is the Partner-in-Charge of Higher Education Consulting Practice of Coopers & Lybrand. Her career has been devoted to helping institutions respond to external and internal challenges through administrative restructuring and reengineering. She has also led enterprise-wide benchmarking and restructuring in universities. Her publications include *Performance Measurement Systems in Higher Education* and *Business Process Redesign in Higher Education*, both published by NACUBO. She wrote a chapter on managing transformation in higher education for the John Wiley & Sons, Inc. Book, *Reinventing the University: Managing and Financing Institutions of Higher Education.*

Sarah Vaughn Massy

Sarah Vaughn Massy is Vice President of the Jackson Hole Higher Education Group, a consultancy that provides services to higher education in the areas of academic restructuring, information technology, resource allocation, and quality assurance. In 1995, she directed the Stanford Forum for Higher Education Futures Technology and Restructuring Roundtable. She also developed and currently edits its paper series, *Executive Strategies*, in collaboration with the National Association of College and University Business Officers (NACUBO). Other clients have included Washington State University, the University of Pennsylvania, Stanford University, the Student Loan Marketing Association, and the Association of Governing Boards of Universities and Colleges.

William F. Massy

William Massy is Codirector of the Stanford Forum for Higher Education Futures. He has had a distinguished career as a university professor and administrator for over 25 years. He currently is President of The Jackson Hole Higher Education Group and Senior Vice President of P.R. Taylor Associates. During his 14-year tenure as Stanford University's Vice President for Business and Finance and Chief Financial Officer, he developed financial management and planning tools that have become standard in the field. Prior to joining the central administration, Massy earned tenure as a professor in the Graduate School of Business where he also held positions as director of the doctoral program and associate dean. He also served Stanford as vice provost for research and acting provost. In 1987 he founded the Stanford Institute for Higher Education Research (SIHER). His recent research has been in the area of faculty roles and responsibilities, academic restructuring, academic information systems, and economic models of institutional finance and departmental behavior. Massy did has graduate work at the Massachusetts Institute of Technology and he holds a baccalaureate from Yale University.

Joel W. Meyerson

Joel Meyerson is Codirector of the Stanford Forum for Higher Education Futures and is chairman emeritus of higher education and nonprofit practices of Coopers & Lybrand. Previously, he codirected the Forum for College Financing at Columbia University. He has served on several advisory panels, including the Massachusetts Board of Regents task forces on capital maintenance and tuition policy, and has taught at the Harvard Institute for Educational Management. He has led major conferences on the globalization and the economics of higher education. Meyerson has edited or coauthored many publications, including *Revitalizing Higher Education*; *Strategy and Finance in Higher Education*; *Productivity and Higher Education*; *Strategic Analysis: Using Comparative Data to Better Understand Your Institution;* and *International Challenges to American Colleges and Universities: Looking Ahead;* and *Higher Education in a Challenging Economy.*

David J. O'Brien

David O'Brien is the Director of the Office of Planning Services at the Stanford University School of Medicine. He has been at the Stanford University Medical Center since 1981. Since early 1994, Mr. O'Brien has lead a project team studying the Medical School's administrative costs and alternative models for the Medical School's administrative organization. In 1996, the School of Medicine's academic leadership approved the project team's recommendations to restructure its research administration organization into a process-based unit and proceed with a four-year plan to develop process-based organizations for the Medical School's other administrative areas. Mr. O'Brien is currently developing the project teams needed to support the Medical School's four-year plans.

Henry E. Riggs

Hank Riggs is President and Professor of Engineering at Harvey Mudd College. Previously, at Stanford University, he served as Vice President for Development and Chairman of the Department of Industrial Engineering and Engineering Management. Riggs is Recipient of Tau Beta Pi Award for Outstanding Teaching and the Walter J. Gores Award for Excellence in Teaching. Riggs has also been President and Chief

Executive Officer, Icore Industries; Vice President–Finance, Measure Corporation, and; Industrial Economist, Stanford Research Institute. Riggs has authored several books and articles including *Financial and Cost Analysis* (Wiley, 1994), *Managing High-Technology Companies* (Van Nostrand Reinhold, 1983), *Accounting: A Survey* (McGraw-Hill, 1981), "Are Merit Scholarships Threatening the Future of Private Colleges?" (*Trusteeship*, Association of Governing Boards, May/June, 1994) and "Fund-Raising Lessons from High-Tech Marketing" (*Harvard Business Review*, 1986).

Jon C. Strauss

Jon Strauss is President Emeritus of Worcester Polytechnic Institute, where he led the transformation from an engineering college to a technical university. Presently, he is Vice President and Chief Financial Officer of the Howard Huges Medical Institute. Previously, he served as Senior Vice President for Administration at the University of Southern California and Vice President for Budget and Finance at the University of Pennsylvania. He has also been professor of computer science at Washington University and Carnegie Mellon University. Strauss has served as a director of several companies, including Computervision Corporation, Wyman-Gordon Company, and the Massachusetts Biotechnology Research Institute. He is also a member of the Visiting Committee, MIT Undergraduate Education and Student Affairs. Strauss is the author of many articles and chapters on computer modeling and simulation and budgeting and planning.

Stephen Joel Trachtenberg

Stephen Joel Trachtenberg has been president of The George Washington University since 1988. He came to GWU from the University of Hartford (CT), where he had been President for eleven years. Before assuming the presidency of Hartford, Trachtenberg served eight years at Boston University as Vice President for Academic Services and Academic Dean of the College of Liberal Arts. Earlier, in Washington, DC, he was a Special Assistant for two years to the U.S. Education Commissioner, Department of Health, Education and Welfare. He has been an attorney and a Professor of Public Administration. In 1994, he published *Speaking His Mind* (ACE/Oryx Press), a collection of his essays on the state of higher education. He is coeditor of the book *The Art of Hiring in America's Colleges & Universities* (Prometheus Books, 1993) and appeared in *Productivity and Higher Education* published by Peterson's in 1992. He serves on the National Collegiate Athletic Association (NCAA) Presidents Commission, the Board of the Chief of Naval Operations (CNO) Executive Panel, and is a director of two New York Stock Exchange-listed public companies.